The Economics of Intangible Investment

NEW DIRECTIONS IN MODERN ECONOMICS
General Editor: Malcolm C. Sawyer,
Professor of Economics, University of Leeds

New Directions in Modern Economics presents a challenge to orthodox economic thinking. It focuses on new ideas emanating from radical traditions including post-Keynesian, Kaleckian, neo-Ricardian and Marxian. The books in the series do not adhere rigidly to any single school of thought but attempt to present a positive alternative to the conventional wisdom.

A list of published titles in this series is printed at the end of this volume.

The Economics of
Intangible Investment

Elizabeth Webster

*Research Fellow, Melbourne Institute of Applied Economic and
Social Research, University of Melbourne, Australia*

NEW DIRECTIONS IN MODERN ECONOMICS

Edward Elgar
Cheltenham, UK • Northampton, MA, USA

332.6
W37e

© Elizabeth Webster 1999

Published by
Edward Elgar Publishing Limited
Glensanda House
Montpellier Parade
Cheltenham
Glos GL50 1UA
UK

Edward Elgar Publishing, Inc.
136 West Street
Suite 202
Northampton
Massachusetts 01060
USA

. A catalogue record for this book
is available from the British Library

Library of Congress Cataloguing in Publication Data

Webster, Elizabeth, 1957–
    The economics of intangible investment / Elizabeth Webster.
        (New directions in modern economics)
    Includes bibliographical references and index.
    1. Investments. 2. Capital. 3. Risk. 4. Uncertainty.
I. Title. II. Series.
HG4515.W43 1999
332.6—dc21   98–53755
                                                                              CIP

ISBN 1 85898 858 6

Printed and bound in Great Britain by Bookcraft (Bath) Ltd.

For Dick

Contents

List of Figures

List of Tables

Acknowledgements

I would like to thank Geoff Harcourt and Robert Dixon for valuable comments and sensible ideas, the Australian Research Council for funding to complete the empirical work in Chapter 6, Geoff Meeks, Malcolm Sawyer and David Johnson for useful suggestions on an early draft and Dick Gross for stock market advice and enthusiastic encouragement. Finally, Joanne Loundes for assistance with compiling the stock market data. All of course, are absolved from any errors contained herein.

1 Introduction

If, as the physicists tell us, the amount of physical matter in the world is fixed, then improvements to our material circumstance can be only wrought through our ability to transform this matter. What distinguishes these abilities and subsequently what allows for differing increments of value, are our capabilities, skills and understandings. The more we know and understand about our physical environment, the less we depend upon our own physical exertion for this transformation process and subsequently the more important our intangible capital, that is, our insights and understanding, becomes. Not only are the individual talents and bits of knowledge important, but so is our capacity to synchronise these components. Non-market networks and workplace organisation in concert with the invisible hand make the 'whole' surpass the sum of the parts.

The significance of intangible skills, both social and individual, was recognised by some, but not all, early political economists. Marshall, for example, believed that non-material wealth was more important than material wealth. He exemplified this by noting that the waste of knowledge following the fall of the Roman Empire took centuries to rebuild while material destruction arising from wars is generally replenished within decades.[1] Despite Marshall's even handed approach to the origins of wealth, the institutionalised procedure developed over the twentieth century has been to treat fixed capital investment as the dominant source of future wealth. In reality, however, this represents only one part of the wealth creation chain for intangible capital is both an input into the tangible capital industry as well as a direct input into the production and delivery of consumables. Nevertheless, it is easy to see why fixed capital accumulation acquired priority status. In a discipline fixated with measurement, tangible capital has excellent properties. We can objectively determine that it exists, it can be stored for use at later occasions and it can be legally sold and valued.

This analytic short cut feels plausible when some sort of representative production line technology dominates our perceptions of the economy. However, the treatment of labour and capital as separate means of production is becoming so conceptually blurred that a labour-as-capital (and an organisation-as-capital) factor, intangible capital, has been created. Evidence from the management and human resources sciences indicates that many firms have become profitable simply because of their investment in the knowledge and abilities of their workforce and their mode of workplace organisation. While there is an established literature which deals with marketing, education, training, foreign investment, innovation, management and workplace organisation, there have been few attempts to identify and analyse their common attributes.

It is not totally clear why there is now an embryonic and belated recognition of intangible forms of capital in the literature.[2] It may be because there has been a growth in intangible investments relative to tangible investments over time, or because intangible capital has become more complex and accordingly, interesting to analyse. Alternatively, it may have arisen because expenditure on intangible capital has been shifting from households to firms. Traditionally, most intangible investment has been financed by households by way of the education and cultural socialisation of children. Economists tend to shy away from issues involving work and consumption within households. However when a process falls under the province of the firm, it produces conceptual conundrums economists warm towards such as appropriability, job tenure, saleability and price volatility.

As an outlay made with the prospect of a future return, intangible investment must clearly be discussed under the general investment umbrella. However, because intangible investments have distinct qualities with distinct implications for the firm and for the economy, they cannot be simply swept into the same symbol as tangible capital. This book examines the process by which firms accumulate intangible capital assets using a post-Keynesian perspective. It differs from any discussions of the topic which follow a mainstream supply dominated perspective. Under the latter, investment is implicitly limited to efforts and exertions that boost the productive capacity of the firm. All investments are assumed to create positive use-values. By contrast, a post-Keynesian or demand dominated approach assumes that firm originating investments are motivated to enhance profits (by way of exchange-values not use-values) and to gain control over the business environment.

Viewed in this way, intangible investment by firms can be driven by three possible motives. First, it can be undertaken to enhance the firm's productive capacity – similar to traditional intangible investment. Second, it can be used as a competitive weapon, and third, it can be used by the firm to contain its level of fundamental uncertainty over its internal and external environment. A firm's investment does not have to be productive in the conventional sense to pay off. Goods and services that attract a high market value do not necessarily have a high use value and vice versa. Intangible investment expenditure, however, like tangible expenditure, will always affect the level of aggregate demand and thus the macroeconomy. Unlike tangible capital however, it has different effects on the firm's retained earnings and its level of mortgagable assets and consequently its future ability to investment.

The greatest single peculiarity of intangible capital, which distinguishes it from tangible capital, is its nexus with labour. A large portion of intangible capital is embodied in labour and the values of items which are not, such as patents and mining leases, depend heavily on the skill of labour to interpret and employ them. This fusion with skilled labour gives intangible capital four notable qualities. First and obviously, labour cannot be owned, sold and mortgaged. Second, labour is innately heterogeneous. It cannot be uniformly mass-produced like physical capital. Third, humans are more volatile and unpredictable than machines. The laws of physics are more regular than the laws of psychology and sociology. And finally, labour appreciates with usage and is a highly malleable factor of production which can metamorphose in many ways. By contrast, physical capital depreciates with usage and each single entity is usually limited to defined tasks.

Our account of the nature of intangible capital will proceed as follows. Chapters 2 and 3 discuss the historical and contemporary conceptions of investment and capital. Intangible capital has crept into the literature under separate and disassociated strands as marketing, training, human capital, innovation and management science. Chapters 4 and 5 discuss the two additional motives, referred to above which drive firms to invest in intangible forms of capital. Chapter 6 examines Australian time series data to test for whether there exists a trend in the level of intangible enterprise investment and capital. Chapters 7 and 8 explore options for microeconomic and macroeconomic models of the investment decision. We conclude with some implications for other areas of economics.

Notes

[1] Marshall ([1890], 1920, 56–8, 138–9, 206–8, 236, 341–2, 411, 546, 611, 625, 780, [1919], 1923, 593).

[2] There has been an annual doubling of papers on intangible capital and investment each year (but from a small base) in the economic and accounting literature according to the *Journal of Economic Literature*.

2 Historic Conception of Investment and Capital

Introduction

Knowledge, the most elementary intangible capital asset, land and labour are the three primary factors of production. Without knowledge, declared Menger, there cannot be goods for we cannot distinguish nutritious from poisonous berries. Without land there are no berries and without labour there are no means of harvesting them (cited in Loasby 1991, 28). In early times it is probable that the acquisition of knowledge capital was due to chance, creative tradespeople or travellers from outside the region (Dosi 1988, 1135–50). As civilisation prospered, knowledge was pursued by gentlemen philosophers who codified and enhanced it as a science. Subsequently, commercial businesses have come to recognise that deliberate investment in intangibles could also be a profitable activity, just as hunter-gatherer communities before them had come to recognise the value of systematic production of tangible capital.

The classical distinction between capital and capital goods tends to be fudged by twentieth century economists. The former is a (wage) fund or monetary advance while the latter comprised the 'concrete' capital, which resulted from the expenditure of this fund. With respect to investment and capital early debates within the economic and political economy literature have been over the scope of goods included within the stock of capital and by implication investment, the relationship between investment and capital and the determination of the normal or required rate of profit.[1]

In this chapter we review the historical development of the notions of capital and investment. While they have been implicitly framed with reference (in most cases) to tangible capital, the same issues present themselves when we try to form a clear picture of what is, and is not, intangible investment and capital.

The scope of capital goods

The assumption that investments only entail activities that create tangible commodities can be traced to *The Wealth of Nations*. Smith ([1776], 1976, 351) argued that only efforts of labour expended in the production of durable tangible commodities could be accumulated and stored for use on other occasions.[2] He rarely referred to investment *per se*,[3] but defined the accumulation of capital in relation to either an increase of fixed (equipment) or circulating capital (inventories) ([1776], 1976, 302–7). Although he mentioned in passing that fixed capital might include 'acquired and useful talents' he did not follow this idea through. In substance, accumulation referred to stocks of physical *goods*.[4]

Smith ([1776], 1976, 351–2) was aware of the importance of knowledge enhancement as a contributor to economic growth, but Marshall developed the ideas more fully and gave it considerable room in *Principles of Economics*. He considered that only labour and land (gifts of nature) were primary factors of production, but stocks of produced material and immaterial goods (the latter being acquired knowledge and business organisation) were also included in aggregate productive assets and wealth ([1890], 1920, 56–8, 138–9, 341–2, 411, 625). Both were the outcome of investment activities although the household accepted responsibility for 'the most valuable investment of all', the education of children ([1890], 1920, 661 and also 206–8, 236, 564). Of the two forms of capital, he considered immaterial capital to be the more important ([1890], 1920, 138 [1919], 1923, 593).

Despite the dominant status given by Marshall to immaterial (intangible) capital, subsequent generations of scholars, especially those working in macroeconomic theory, marginalised it and investments became synonymous with additions to the stock of tangible goods. The macroeconomic theories of Robinson, Hicks, Solow, Samuelson and Kalecki are prime examples. A common view of technical progress, and often by implication workplace reorganisation, workforce training or additional sales promotion efforts, were that they were costlessly and exogenously acquired features of firms and markets. With the exception of Schumpeter who recognised that profit-bearing investments may include intangibles such as research and development, innovations and new products, most authors did not treat expenditure on intangible capital as integral to the investment decision.[5]

Additional debates in this area were concerned with whether capital should include both durable household items (consumption capital) and goods, which aid labour in production plus finished and unfinished goods (instrumental capital). Jevons believed it should although Marshall thought that including the former burdens analysis with 'incessant enumeration of details of secondary importance' ([1890], 1920, 78).[6]

Finally, there was discussion over whether investment was the whole of the working capital required in each period to allow capitalists to undertake production or merely a change in the level of working capital relative to the previous period (and thus a change in inventories). According to Robinson ([1956], 1966, 41), who appeared to have the last word on this issue, only the last definition is valid. Since all sales of goods are a disinvestment, it is a legitimate simplification in a short-period steady state to speak of sales at any moment being matched by production.

The chosen length of the unit period determines whether sales equal purchases of inputs in any one period. Only part of working capital that contributed to a build up (or decline) in inventories should be counted as investment and the total advance of money (which has command over resources) needed to cover any period's production does not in its entirety constitute investment. Using the same rationale replacement investment is similar to working capital purchases in a steady state. However, she notes that in reality technological progress does not allow us to clearly distinguish replacement from net investments.

Relationship between investment and aggregate capital

A frequently implied notion accepted by both Harrod and Kalecki, is that investment less depreciation defines the change in the stock of capital goods. Under this view, capital is a backward-looking measure equal to the compounded sum of past investments less wear and tear.

The less popular, but more logically appealing definition of the change in stock of capital, is the forward looking measure, the present value of future net income (or quasi-rents) derived from the use of capital at hand. Investment expenditure, on the other hand, is the sum of what firms' outlay on building up their capital and the two are not directly related. This forward measure of capital depends critically on expectations and is unashamedly a value measure of either a collection of capital goods or a single item. It was the concept used by both Keynes ([1936], 1973, Ch. 11) and von Hayek (1941, 13). Investment expenditure may *influence* the change in the capital stock by affecting profits and thus expectations of quasi-rents but it does not determine it. The happy day when the two are equal is Robinson's Golden Age and Harrod's equilibrium warranted rate of growth.

Regardless of the fact that the backward measure uses relative prices to add and subtract the different vintages of capital goods, it is still trying to squeeze a quasi-physical notion of capital into the meaning of aggregate capital goods. Most late nineteenth and early twentieth century economists were aware that an aggregate measure of 'capital' could not exist without introducing money values.[7] However, it was unclear how they could rationalise the physical marginal productivity angle derived from partial analysis, with the classical notion of the economy tending towards a long-period equilibrium position based on a uniform rate of profit on capital. A physical concept of capital only has meaning within a firm or group of homogenous firms and can be conceived on a macro level in a very imprecise way. Yet the notion of a rate of profit is very precise. Either the physical notion of aggregate capital or the notion of a long-period equilibrium position had to be sacrificed.

Walras tried to marry the two concepts together in his General Equilibrium model. However his set of equations, even when allowance is made for the production of capital goods, are still claimed to be inconsistent (that is, over determined, see Garegnani (1987) and Eatwell (1987)). Despite this, many modern textbooks are cast in the Walrasian tradition and proceed to define the aggregate capital stock in the backward looking quasi-physical way.[8]

Conclusion

Although the economic role of investment in immaterial goods was a strong and recurring theme throughout Marshall's *Principles of Economics* it has taken nearly a century for these ideas to attract attention in macroeconomics.[9] In particular the explicit restriction of investment and capital to tangible capital goods by Marshall's academic descendants is curious. We find, in the following chapter, that the broader and more accurate conception of investment which includes the creation of both tangible and intangible goods was first taken seriously by management theoreticians and subsequently by microeconomists working in the industrial and labour market spheres, rather than by macroeconomists for whom investment is a central concern.

Schumpeter ([1911], 1934, 116, italicised in the original) has argued that '*Capital is nothing but the lever by which the entrepreneur subjects to his control the concrete goods which he needs, nothing but a means of diverting the factors of production to new uses, or of dictating a new direction to production*'. Had Schumpeter's definition of the capital fund held currency, then it is questionable whether intangible capital assets would have been excluded from the meaning of capital goods for so long.

Notes

[1] The required rate of profit is the expected rate of return firms require before they will embark upon an investment project.

[2] Of course this was an advance on the physiocrats who only included agricultural produce and the mechantilists before them who believed that a country's wealth (assets) only include precious metals and jewels (Pasinetti 1981, 5).

3   Investment is spoken of as the provision of finance, the contribution capitalists make to the production process that enables them to receive profit (Smith [1776], 1976, 63).

4   It is likely that this was also because in the eighteenth century most services were either produced for households (and were thus consumption goods) or for the government (Smith [1776], 1976, 351–2).

5   Schumpeter ([1911], 1934, 65–8). There were some other exceptions. Knight ([1921], 1946, 172, 341) speaks of firms' investments in knowledge creation. Boulding (1950, 28) mentions how workforce morale and other goodwill items should be included in a firm's capital. Wood (1975) builds the need for finance for sales promotion into his model.

6   However, as he notes (Marshall [1890], 1920, 785), this gives rise to certain anomalies. For example, if two producers of household capital items desire the services of each other's goods, the amount of capital in the economy varies according to whether the goods are sold or leased to each other.

7   Kurz (1987, 81) refers to Jevons, Böhm-Barwerk and Wicksell. Keynes ([1936], 1973, 43) is clearly of this view also.

8   See for example Sargent (1987, 7).

9   Loasby (1991) has consistently drawn attention to Marshall's views on these matters.

3 Contemporary Conception of Investment

Introduction

There has been a modest number of papers in the past few decades which recognise intangible investments as a discrete category,[1] but the greater part of the history of intangible capital has been discussed separately by distinct branches of microeconomics under the topics of innovation, advertising, education and training, organisational change and rent-seeking behaviour. According to Abramovitz (1993) the shifting emphasis in the literature towards intangible capital reflects the changing character of technical progress over time.[2] During the nineteenth century new technologies were largely embodied in fixed capital while this century they have been embodied in intangibles and labour (Kendrick 1972, 1994; Auerbach 1988, Ch. 5).

The appropriability of benefits is a critical issue for investment in both tangible and intangible goods. However, while legal constraints and insurance enhance the appropriability of tangible *capital* the appropriability problem associated with intangible capital assets is primarily due to the inability to assign property rights over persons. It is not due to the public good nature of intangible goods as is often assumed, for example, by Romer (1986, 1990) and Grossman and Helpman (1991).[3]

Intangible capital are excludable assets whose value critically hinges on the retention of skilled staff. However, intangible *inputs* are not necessarily excludable precisely because their non-excludability makes them inputs rather than assets.[4] An idea that can be easily copied or made redundant by rivals will be viewed by the firms as an intermediate input whose value is used up within one period. A capital asset by definition must have some provision which prevents it being copied or taken from within the firm. It is a means of production whose value, that is, ability to attract profits, lasts beyond the current period. Intermediate inputs or current expenses are consumed within their period of purchase.

Whether an asset or an intermediate input, tangible and intangible goods have no value to the firm independently from their ability to generate profits (see von Hayek 1941, 331). Accordingly, both intangible inputs and capital are rivalrous goods whose value depreciates by joint consumption during a given period. While an idea or a discovery is non-rivalrous in its use value that is value to the consumer, its *exchange* value is rivalrous. However, repeated uses of intangible capital over multiple time periods are not necessarily rivalrous.

We find that when we broaden our notion of investment goods beyond plant and equipment, there exist several motives for undertaking investment. While both expenditure on tangible and intangible goods are undertaken by firms to reduce costs of production and increase productive capacity, they can also embrace the broader functions of enhancing demand for the firm's existing products, discovering new profitable areas of expansion and mitigating market risk and uncertainty associated with the firm's activities. According to both Penrose and Auerbach the discovery of new profitable areas and the ability of a firm to change its environmental constraints comprise the essential spirit of the competitive process (Penrose [1959], 1980; Auerbach 1988). Furthermore, Dixon has argued that capital accumulation in the broadest sense is the means by which business can exercise power (Dixon 1986, 587–9). In the context of our discussion, this means that by raising demand, reducing risk and discovering new markets, expenditure by the firm on intangible goods may directly create new intangible capital assets. In practice the latter are often partly valued by the firm under the 'catch all' category, goodwill.

This chapter provides a discussion of the meaning of investment, the types of investment goods and the nature of the distinction between current and capital expenditures, the three firm level motives for investment activity and evidence for the importance of the intangible investments. It refers almost exclusively to the microeconomic investment decision.

Abstract notion

In *The Theory of Interest* Irving Fisher (1930, 114) defined saving or investment as the postponement of current consumption for deferred enjoyment. Similarly Marshall ([1890], 1920, 233) believed that 'abstinence from the particular act of consumption [would] increase the accumulation of wealth'. Investments were 'human efforts and sacrifices, devoted mainly to securing benefits in the future rather than in the present' ([1890], 1920, 787).[5] For our purpose, we will assume that investment activity involves the production, at a cost, of an asset which is expected to yield a future stream of positive income. To understand our concept of investment, it should be clearly distinguished from consumption, saving and lending.

Investment and consumption

Inherent in the distinction between consumption and investment is a notion of how quickly effort is converted into enjoyment.[6] Practical difficulties in measuring and recording the temporal conversion of these efforts has led to the convention within economic theory established by Marshall that purchases by households signify 'consumption' and purchases by firms signify 'investment' ([1890], 1920, 76–8).

Investment and saving

Early economists reasoned that if investing was to abstain from current consumption, then it was the same activity as saving. However, it was realised during the 1920s that this relationship need only hold in aggregate since it is possible for different parties to undertake either saving or investment without the other. It was then established that saving was the abstinence from immediate consumption, while investment was the expenditure on a good or service that promises to deliver this deferred enjoyment at a later date. The motives, which determine each activity, are distinct and not related (Keynes [1936], 1973, 21). Only in the case of a firm or household which uses its own funds to acquire or produce a good which provides future services (that is, house or plant and equipment), may saving and investment occur as the same act.

Investment and intertemporal trade

An individual or firm may change their intertemporal psychic or material income by borrowing from or lending to another party or person. Fisher called this 'a trade with mankind' rather than an investment which is a 'trade with the environment' (1930, 181). If we allow for the accumulation of foreign reserves, lending may constitute a form of national investment. However, taking the world economy as a whole, lending and borrowing between parties while perhaps enhancing social wellbeing, does not constitute necessarily investment or saving. Aggregate saving and consumption do not change in each time period.

Types of firm investment

In the context of the firm, investment is an outlay made in the expectation of future profits and the scope of relevant capital naturally extends beyond plant and equipment. A firm may acquire capital to enhance profitability by extending its knowledge base, its control over its environment and its productive capacity. We will call 'capacity capital', capital which raises the maximum level of production per period of the firm. 'knowledge capital' those intangible assets which improve our understanding of the market and profit opportunities; and 'control capital', those assets which enable the firm to both raise the firm's demand curve by increasing the firm's market power and lower its cost curve by improving production efficiency. Clearly some types of investment affect more than one type of asset. For example, a process innovation can both promote cost efficiency and increase the firm's capacity. However, we will ask the reader to abstract from this joint production aspect and assume for our discussion in later chapters that we can assign, on a microeconomic basis, a functional relationship between the type of investment activity and the designated asset.

The implied rate of economic depreciation (including obsolescence) determines whether a commodity constitutes a current expense (that is an input) or an asset. When production is being matched by sales at any point in time, only a change in the stocks of intermediate inputs and not the whole expense constitute an investment. Thus a change in the level of working capital or investment inputs is an investment or disinvestment.

Capacity capital arises from all investments which increase the rate at which firms may potentially produce. This is not restricted to tangible plant and equipment. Investments to enlarge the productive potential of existing tangible capital and the existing workforce, such as a more skilled and proficient workforce and a more streamlined system of organisation, will raise the maximum level of productive capacity in the firm.

Knowledge capital refers to the discovery of new, or acquisition of existing knowledge concerning product design, production process, marketing, distribution methods (acquired either by formal research and development teams or via on the job learning and innovating),[7] and general market information on rivals, suppliers, consumers, market segments, distribution channels and government (See Hymer [1960], 1976, 41–6; Arrow [1974a] 1984, 162, [1974b], 1984, 173; Magee 1977; Rugman 1981; Fröhlich 1989; Francis 1989; Karlsson 1989; Ray *et al* 1989; Cantwell 1989; Porter 1990; Ch. 1; Morck and Yeung 1991). According to both von Hayek ([1946] 1949, 94–6) and Richardson ([1960], 1990, *xiv*), firms regard one of their basic problems as the discovery of the position and shape of their demand or cost functions, especially the knowledge relating to the activities of others. Acquisition of information is a prerequisite for acquiring power and reducing the effects of uncertainty. Out-of-equilibrium agents need information on more that just prices and quantities as changing relative prices imply a need for information on new uses for products and inputs (Arrow 1959).

The difference between information and knowledge is crucial here. A great deal of information is free or obtainable at little overt cost from libraries, information systems and the public media. It is, however, the ability to employ this information in an intelligent way, to apply generally known facts and principles to new areas, and to select and process information for relevance, that constitutes knowledge (Lachmann 1986, 46, 51). To undertake this transformation from information into knowledge, a firm needs knowledge capital, that is, a core group of core workers who are experienced and educated in the how, what, where and why of information selection and use.

The efficient acquisition and effective use of existing knowledge is enhanced by the education, training and industry experience of the potential workforce, all of which are costly and time consuming. New knowledge is not necessarily more valuable than existing knowledge for the latter has the advantage of having already been tested in the market place.[8] Much critical management knowledge is tacit and must be acquired on-the-job. Time and expense are needed to maintain and develop the intangible industry network capital (Eliasson 1988, 81; Johansson and Mattsson 1988, 295). The view that the successful application of new technologies depends heavily on the ability of in-house employees to understand the process finds support from a broad range of empirical studies (Caves 1982a, 201, 204–7; Freeman 1974, 247, 263; Teece 1977, 243, 250, 259; Dosi 1988, 1125–35 and Porter 1990, Ch. 2).

Collectively, *control capital* is a device which enables the firm to control input markets, control the quality and quantity of work effort within the firm and control product markets. Management desires to control workers, the entrepreneur desires to control management, shareholders desire to control the entrepreneur and everyone wants to control customers and rivals. Decisions within the firm can be made by all three tiers of authority and we expect to find measures to effect all three forms of control in existence. The greater are uncertainty and the importance of sunk costs, the greater are the potential costs of ruinous price wars and aggressive union demands and the greater is the need for the firm to establish both internal and external market discipline. The acquisition of knowledge capital (and inputs) is generally antecedent to the acquisition of control capital.

To be able to exploit an opportunity, we need, as a minimum, authority over the firm's internal environment. The manager needs to be able to direct how, when and what the firms will produce next. Expansion and the ability to dominate the external environment by acquiring more resources, generally involves a loss of internal control by the original owner(s) as new share issues or loans are undertaken. Mergers are primarily about the raiding firm's desire to prevent becoming a victim firm and being controlled by another firm (Hay and Morris 1991, 498, 524–26, 530). Achieving a suitable balance between internal and external control remains a key decision for the entrepreneur or manager.

A regular level of debt commitment arises from shareholders' desire for control. To invest and acquire market control, without loss of internal control due to an expansion of the equity base, businesses borrow. However, the introduction of fixed debt outlays raises the possibility of bankruptcy and this in turn has implications for the motive to invest.

Control capital can be divided into organisation, market access and rent-seeking capital. Organisation goods affect the industrial harmony and efficiency of management and employees in the workplace (Marshall [1890], 1920, 266; Doeringer and Terkla 1990). They impact on absenteeism and turnover, morale and the degree of acceptance by employees of change, skill transfer and subsequently total factor productivity. Co-ordination is crucial for efficiency and the organisational system is crucial for co-ordination (Nelson and Winter 1982, Ch. 5; Porter 1990, Ch. 2; Best 1990, 11, 60). According to many management and industrial economists, organisational restructuring has become a major instrument of competition and control and a determinant of information flows and productivity changes within the firm (Arrow [1974b], 1984, 178–79; Dosi 1988, IIId; Hamel and Prahalad 1988; Eliasson 1988, 61; Dunning 1988; Adams 1989, 149–50; Ray *et al.* 1989; Borner 1989, 67; Best 1990, 11–14; Moir 1990, 105; Chandler and Hikino 1990, 24, 594; Porter 1990, Ch. 2; Odagiri 1992, Ch. 3).[9] Without an appropriate organisation, Best argues that it is not possible for firms to introduce new processes, forms of innovation and improvements to product quality.[10]

Organisational goods may extend beyond the firm to include local networks. Marshall's theory of the benefits of co-operation and division of labour between firms and industries has been extended by several authors who contend that a degree of collusion and networking between firms assists the diffusion of knowledge and thus the efficiency of firms within the network compared to elsewhere (Marshall [1890], 1920, 255–66, 271, see also Young 1928; Loasby 1982, 1983; Johansson and Mattsson 1988; Porter 1990, Ch. 1; Best 1990, 16, 38–41, 233).

Market access goods refer to established footholds in markets which may have been gained by the establishment or dominance of distribution networks, successful education of consumers with respect to a new product and other efforts undertaken to develop demand for a product (such as prolonged subsidisation of the full cost of a product) (Marshall 1890, 396; Rothschild 1947, 317–18; Slatter 1977, 40; Hamel and Prahalad 1988; Araujo *et al* 1989; Cantwell 1989; Porter 1990, Ch. 2; Chandler and Hikino 1990, 40). According to Demsetz, reputation is an asset because information is not free and the consumer relies upon it to reduce his or her uncertainty (Demsetz 1982, 51).

Rent-seeking goods refer to deliberate efforts by the firm to reduce competition against it by obtaining greater control over supplies and distribution, mergers, acquisitions or strategic alliances and changing government regulations.[11] It may seem odd to include these as investment goods, but in a demand-side theory, there is nothing that requires that an investment be intrinsically productive at an aggregate level. All that is required is that it contribute to expenditure and compete for sales revenue.

Current or capital expense?

To include the creation of the above goods as an investment activity, we have to determine whether a good is an asset because it produces a stream of services to the user beyond the immediate period or it is a consumption good or piece of working capital because its services are used within a 'single period'. Clearly almost all items of 'fixed' capital could be classified as working capital (inputs) if we define the period to be very long. In post-Keynesian theories such as Kalecki's models, the unit period, which is the time it takes to reconsider the investment decision on the basis of realised profits, is not excessively long.

While we can see tangible goods being transformed during the production process, the classification of intangibles is more subjective and more continuous as it relies in many cases on economic obsolescence. The effects of advertising expenditure may be gained quickly but a small trickle of benefits may still flow for a long time (Chamberlin [1933], 1962, 133–35; Kaldor 1950–51; Comanor and Wilson 1979; Telser 1961; Hirschey 1982; Morck and Yeung 1992). Expenditures on knowledge creation, workplace harmony, market access and rent-seeking gains may also have a stream of returns which is skewed to the right when mapped against time. These goods yield services which either reduce costs of production, expand capacity, change market boundaries, shift a firm's final demand curve or reduce firm risk and uncertainty. If these goods are circumstance specific or rival firms retaliate by emulation, then single items will depreciate quickly, making them intermediate inputs rather than capital assets.

We can be more confident however, that *experience* in generating knowledge and acting upon that knowledge to undertake improvements to control goods, is an asset (Caves 1982a, 3–7). Experience is of course embodied in labour. Experience is knowing what information to seek next, the position of having met many similar situations before, being able to problem-solve in context and learning to make on-the-job adaptations as circumstances change. While specific advice maybe an intermediate input, the ability to generalise and generate new and useful advice is a durable asset. Experienced staff represent an investment because they form a perpetual source of future benefits, the production of intangible current inputs. Similarly, possession or access to institutional arrangements that give the firm control over its internal and external environments is also an asset.

Firms may invest in human intangible capital by formal work related training, on-the-job training or learning-by-doing. Unlike tangible capital which are subject to 'user-cost' (Keynes [1936], 1973, 52–3), the more these intangible capital are used to produce intangible inputs, the greater is their value.[12] We must speak instead of user benefit not user cost. Intangible capital may be produced both as joint products with normal output during normal productive activity, or as the result of deliberate decisions by the firm.

According to Kirzner (1979) only predictable learning can be handled within a cost–benefit framework and thus packaged and sold. Unplanned knowledge can only be acquired on-the-job. These jointly acquired intangible capital will be firm-specific to the extent that each firm's productive activity differs and to the extent that each firm's organisation encourages learning and alert behaviour by the workforce. The more efficient is the firm in promoting the transmission of intra-firm knowledge the greater is the value of these intangible capital. Intra-firm knowledge transmission is of course one of the salient features of Internal Labour Markets (ILMs) (Caves 1982a, 3, 10). There is no neat way to dichotomise these intangible goods into intermediate or investment goods, but the discussion within this book will, unless otherwise specified, refer to the asset component of an intangible commodity.

Motives for investment

When our notion of investment is considered, it is clear that, at its most general level, a firm's investment expenditure will only be motivated by the expectation of a profitable return. This motive may be expressed as three intermediate motives

- first, the desire to passively respond to opportunities which macroeconomic growth offers, by increasing the level of productive capacity,

- secondly, the desire to reduce uncertainty over future outcomes which subsequently allows the firm to better direct its investment activities, and
- finally, the need to aggressively compete against market competitors by keeping up with standard business practices and by developing devices which give the firm a specific cost or demand advantage.

All three motives can involve the creation of both tangible and intangible capital. A firm may expand productive capacity by acquiring plant and equipment, reorganising the workplace and reforming the system of industrial relations or by retraining the workforce. The competitive motive also involves investment in both tangible and intangible capital. Upholding state-of-the-art industry standards may involve purchasing the latest plant and equipment. However, developing new and more effective business practices often involves a large portion of intangible investments. These may include the development of work teams who are skilled and experienced at developing new products and process technologies, new forms of marketing and distribution networks and new ways of containing competition by rent-seeking measures.

When significant assets are bound up in the particular team of labour and the workplace culture, the firm will endeavour to achieve high staff retention and reproduction rates over the relevant set of skilled employees. The ILM is the classic organisational feature which has the properties of retaining and training enough managers to perpetuate the ethos, skills and specific work-related practices. We expect to find this workplace organisation, or separate critical features (long-service leave provisions, seniority rules, career paths, wages above opportunity cost, job security, employee benefits) in firms with larger endowments of intangible capital. The higher is the expenditure on intangible commodities, the greater is the loss to the firm of skills and knowledge through staff turnover. [13]

The firm's uncertainty over the dispersion and scope of possible outcomes may be circumscribed by the acquisition of knowledge and control capital. These assets should reduce the sensitivity of a firm's demand to rival manoeuvres and exogenous events. According to Richardson, 'market imperfections' created by intangible investments (not his terminology) are crucial for ensuring enough *certainty* of future demand for the firm's products to allow any form of investment to be undertaken in the first place ([1960], 1990, 14, 23, Ch. 2). In perfect market conditions, this assurance is absent regardless of the number of firms in the market and investment activity by the firm will be a highly hazardous and conjectural affair.

Our brief *a priori* discussion of the ways of satisfying the three motives for investment activity, suggests that competitive conditions and uncertainty involve the creation of a higher portion of intangible to tangible capital, than the productive capacity motive. For clarity, we repeat our conclusion from the previous section. Not all expenditures on intangible goods constitute investment activity. If the value of the good to the firm expires within the period it is created, it is a current expense or an intermediate input. We cannot be sure to what extent the activities referred to above produce capital assets or inputs. However, we will take it as given that for the remainder of this book, we speak only of the investment portion.

Evidence from broader literature

The importance of intangible capital assets is reflected in the behaviour of firms with respect to its foreign direct investment (FDI), its internal labour market and its hiring practices may be responsible for a change to its hiring practices this century. The growth of literature in these areas furnishes us with further evidence of the importance of intangible investment and capital during the latter part of the twentieth century. We consider these in turn.

Foreign direct investment
The internalisation theory argues that the need to fully appropriate the returns to intangible capital is the prime force behind FDI or other forms of firm expansion into segmented product markets. If there is no regular market for intangible capital assets, because of its tacit or firm-specific nature, FDI allows the firms to profitably expand without undermining domestic markets. The benefits from research and development, advertising, management experience, labour relations skills, and market knowledge are more fully exploited. Empirical studies indicate that firms that undertake this activity to increase the appropriability of benefits from intangible assets, receive a capital gain (Hymer [1960], 1976, 25, 41–6; Magee 1977; Grabowski and Mueller 1978; Buckley 1985; Rugman 1981; Morck and Yeung 1991, 1992; Caves 1982a, 9–10, 153, 1982b; Markusen 1995).[14]

Internal Labour Markets
ILMs are hierarchical firm structures specifically designed to reduce labour turnover, enhance the development of firm-specific skills and appropriate the benefits of training and learning-by-doing. The growing importance of ILMs during this century may indicate that these skills are becoming increasingly important to the success of the firm (Doeringer and Piore 1971). As the pace of competition fought via technological development quickens, so does the

value to firms of being able to respond by continually innovating and acquiring knowledge of new ways doing things. However, this propensity depends on the ability of a firm to draw upon its own cumulated experience and knowledge which cannot be effectively codified but resides in the minds of the workforce (Dosi 1988; Porter 1990, Ch. 2).

This does not mean that ILMs never fire their asset and management staff. Organisational change (such as the currently fashionable lean production principles) may require a change in the number and type of asset labour in the same way that firms retire and replace their plant and equipment.

Hiring practices

Much has been written on the causes of the widely observed outward shift of the U–V (unemployment–vacancy) hyperbola mainly in the context of hysteresis and a shifting NAIRU.[15] Effectively it involves premature tightening of labour markets at levels below full-employment. Existing theories explain this by either the labour market scarring effect of prolonged unemployment on potential workers, the importance of firm-specific skills or by a voluntary choice by people for leisure over work (Layard *et al.* 1991, Ch. 1). However, as the U–V relationship did not appear to shift after the high periods of unemployment during the 1930s it is less clear that these factors on their own can offer a full explanation.

The apparently observed hysteresis since the mid-1970s and its absence during the 1930s is theoretically consistent with a positive trend in the importance of intangible capital, especially tacitly acquired capital which can only be acquired on-the-job.[16] As firms' technology (in the broadest sense of the word) and production methods become increasingly firm- and product-specific and dependent on learning by doing, their ability and desire to absorb generally trained outsiders is reduced. Knowing the way the firm, the industry and the market operate have acquired a premium value and this drives a productivity wedge between the unemployed and incumbent employees. Even when the firm desires to increased production due to buoyant product market demand, unemployed outsiders are not a viable input at the going wage rate and the U–V relationship rises. In short, a growth in the importance of intangible capital over the last half of the twentieth century may explain the sudden relevance of Lindbeck and Snower's (1986) insider-outsider phenomenon.

Additionally, the relative cost of appropriating the benefits of intangible capital has been used to explain firm size (Morck and Yeung 1992), the growth of franchises (Caves and Murphy 1976) and merger activity (Magee 1977, 337). The faster growth rate of small firms in the 1980s has been linked with the rising importance of intangible goods in tailoring products more closely to customer needs instead of the use of sophisticated tangible capital and economies of scale. There is some empirical support indicating a positive relationship between intangible investments and firm value (Caves and Murphy 1976; Hirschey 1982; Megna and Klock 1993; Chauvin and Hirschey 1993, White 1995). Business management academics believe that intangible investments, especially those aimed at developing management, professional and technical skills, are so important that they are the principal source of the success of large firms. Success depends on management as agents of change, administrators of complex organisations and processors of information (Chandler and Hikino 1990, 8, 594; Porter 1990, Ch. 2).

Conclusion

Once it is accepted that investment comprises any present outlay which promises to reap a future reward – the field naturally opens to include all varieties of intangible capital such as the acquisition of knowledge, and the ability to control the firm's internal and external environment by changing the organisation, industrial relations system, labour skills and by enhancing market access and protective rent-producing barriers. Intangible investment activities should not be limited to research and development and commercially successful innovations.[17]

Our empirical work in Chapter 6 finds that intangibles currently comprise at least 30 per cent of firms' capital (see Table 6.3). According to Richardson, without some control capital the reliability and certainty of deriving profits from tangible asset investments are heavily undermined (not his terminology).

Almost all empirical tests of the determinants of the aggregate investment equation restrict the dependent variable to tangible investments only, and are thus not properly specified, under our meaning of investment. Even were we to restrict our interest to the productive capacity motive, for example by using some form of accelerator model, activities such as workforce retraining, reorganisation and industrial relations improvements should also be counted as legitimate investments. Econometric estimates, which do not include the full breadth of investment expenditures, are therefore not reliable indicators of the significance of causal factors.

Notes

[1] See Kendrick (1972), Caves and Murphy (1976), Magee (1977), Grabowski and Mueller (1978), Rugman (1981), Hirschey (1982), Caves (1982a), Cantwell (1989), Borner (1989), Megna and Mueller (1989), Doeringer and Terkla (1990), Schreyer and Clarke (1991), Megna and Klock (1993).

[2] Intangible inputs and capital reflect not only a growth in importance of the value to consumers of product design and quality (in preference to *quantity* of goods) but the importance of intangible goods in the production function.

[3] Caves (1982b, 275) and Cantwell (1989, 9–12) actually argue that the cost of technology transfer is significant enough to make knowledge not a public good. We cannot separate creation from use without cost.

[4] The ability of rival firms to overtake and improve on a firm's intangible goods also makes them inputs rather than assets. This is not related to excludability of a particular intangible good.

[5] He believed that both saving and investment were struck as the balance between the loss of satisfaction due to waiting and the expected satisfactions from the fruits of investment.

[6] This temporal difference is also at the heart of the distinction between durable and non-durable capital, that is, inputs and assets.

[7] It is commonly accepted by industrial economists that most technical change is incremental (see Auerbach 1988, 265; Dosi (1988); Ray *et al.* (1989); Myhrman (1989, 47); Cantwell 1989, 2–4, 18).

[8] Franchises are usually sold when there are some successful going concerns. Successful businesses are often established after the first entrepreneur has gone bankrupt trying to commercialise a new idea. The second owner buys the business at a discount, and benefits from the learning experience.

[9] Groenewegen considers organisational development the main form of technological progress during the eighteenth century (cited in Reid 1989, Ch. 9).

[10] Seminar Queen's College, Cambridge May 1995.

[11] Dewey (1969, 118) claims bribes in the form of directorships, consultants fees, and overpayment for services are common ways by which firms encourage other firms not to enter the industry.

[12] According to Polanyi, a tacitly skilled person performs by following a set of rules of which the person is only unconsciously aware. These people inevitably chose similar choices in similar situations, while less skilled people probably deliberate more about the decision (Nelson and Winter 1982, 77, 82).

[13] Freeman (1974, 247) believes that a major form of inter-firm spillover of research and development goods is via staff mobility.

[14] Oddly no mention is made in these studies of the influence access to investment funds has on the choice between FDI and licensing.

[15] NAIRU refers to the non-accelerating inflation rate of unemployment.

[16] Some of these are the insider–outsider theories.

[17] Contemporary applied studies such as Geroski and Walters (1995, 919) have limited themselves to the narrower definition.

4 Uncertainty and Risk

Introduction

In the previous chapter, we argued that the distinction between investment activity and expenditure on intermediate inputs is not defined by type of good being produced or the type of inputs employed in its production. Instead investment goods should be distinguished from immediate inputs by the length of their anticipated profit horizon. If the firm expects that the use of a particular good will provide returns for more than one period, then the good is a capital asset and its creation constitutes an investment. This time horizon distinction is also important in macrodynamic theories because it is the time lag between anticipated and realised profits that produces cumulative investment expenditure levels and cyclical swings in the economy.

The stereotypical notion that plant and equipment constitute the only form of firm capital is clearly at odds with the accepted wisdom in both industrial economics and theories of management science and it is a narrow interpretation of the notion of investment. Under this broader definition, not only are there several motives for investment, but the traditional motive, the requirement for more productive capacity, can be satisfied by both tangible and intangible capital. In the place of more plant and equipment a firm can increase its productive capacity by introducing more efficient forms of workplace organisation and systems of industrial relations, or by retraining the work force.

This productive capacity motive for investment spending is already part of most micro and macro investment theories. Investment is assumed to respond positively as demand for output and profits rise, and decline as they fall. Although important, this motive for investment activity shall be left aside while we examine more thoroughly the two other motives for investment. The next two chapters examine the effects of both product market uncertainty and competitive pressure in determining the level of investment activity.

We begin by establishing postulates governing firms' behaviour; we examine the meaning and causes of risk and uncertainty, some relevant theoretical treatments of uncertainty from the literature, how risk and uncertainty affects the evaluation of investment projects; and the ways firms seek to accommodate their risk and uncertainty. We finish with a short conclusion. We confine our discussion to the level of the firm.

The compulsion to act

Firms do not have motivations. Only people do (Hay and Morris, 1991, 293). When we speak of firm's choices, firm's behaviours or firm's motives, it is a short-cut for referring to the key person(s) who control the relevant decision within the firm. Greed, the so-called self-evident axiom of profit maximisation, is not the only impetus propelling human behaviour. Lust, envy, sloth, self-respect and compassion are conventionally accepted as fundamental to the human condition also.[1] According to Loasby (1983, 117), our positive attributes define the basic values and codes of conduct which a person must cling to in order to still regard him or herself as a worthy person. Since Mill, however, economists have emphasised the profit incentive only as a way of abstracting from these non-economic and non-systematic motives.

Clearly if we are seeking to model the behaviour of the firm as a process played out over sequences of historical time periods, it is desirable if we can reflect the intensity to which the firm pursues profit at the expense of other motives. It is most straightforward to stylise firm's behaviours as outcomes of optimising decisions. Accordingly, we maintain the postulate that the firm seeks to maximise the present value of assets, that is, the expected flow of profits over the long-term. However, we allow the importance of other motives to moderate the allowance firms make for risk-aversion. We may say then, that firms seek to maximise profits *once other factors are accounted for*, and we allow our risk-aversion premium factor, let us call it x, to vary when we want to systematically alter these other factors.

Additionally, we argue that firms use investment as the main instrumental variable for achieving profit maximisation. Specifically investment in control and knowledge capital may achieve this end, first, when cost and demand barriers are endogenous to firm behaviour[2] and secondly, when it enables the firm to increase its confidence over future events or limit the scope of likely outcomes (Knight [1921], 1946, 238–78; Simon [1976], 1979, 81; Lamberton 1972, 260; Dixon 1986; Lavoie 1992, 58). *Ceteris paribus,* we expect that a risk-averse firm will prefer a smaller range of likely outcomes to a wider range.

In static neoclassical competition theories, it is assumed that the intensity of entrepreneurs' internal competitive drive is so great that the firm is almost always at its objectively given profit-maximising position. Potential endogenous barriers and advantages will immediately be exploited by all firms and by implication eradicated. Exogenous barriers remain the sole determinant of market structure and the industry's potential to earn above normal profit. A firm has only to respond to changes in exogenous circumstances by setting prices and quantity according to profit-maximising principles and investing to achieve the implied long-period optimal productive capacity.

Under process theories of competition however, the irreversible nature of investment activity leads the firm to undertake investment as a series of tentative steps towards an uncertain and most likely shifting target of subjective long-run profit-maximising positions. The scope for affecting profits by price variation appears by contrast smaller. Once an investment project is committed, and costs of production and the nature of the product relatively fixed, there is a comparatively narrow range with which the firm can vary price and still cover costs.

The origins of risk and uncertainty

Uncertainty is the 'plurality of those descriptions of the future which the decision-maker looks upon in some degree, as possible' (Shackle [1961–62], 1966, 86). Uncertainty in most contexts excludes actuarial risks.[3] The outcome of a proposed action is considered 'risky' if it arises from situations (or classes of situations) that occur with such frequency that one is able to derive a reliable contingent frequency table for possible outcomes. Fundamentally uncertain outcomes, on the other hand, arise from situations which are so singular or unlike past cases that no estimate which is meaningful or reliable *ex post* can be made. In a trivial sense no situation is ever exactly repeated: we must argue that risk situations occur when the *essentials* of particular circumstance are repeated many times or that the individual does not *believe* that they behold a simple repetition of previous experiences. Many experiences, which we classify as general experience, only appear so in the wisdom of hindsight. When we review a previous situation our broader perspective, especially about what other parties had been thinking and doing at the time, allows greater powers of generalisation.

Uncertainty implies a lack of knowledge, unlike actuarial probability calculations which require the existence of substantial knowledge.[4] Unless situations are repeated many times, it is not possible to test after the event whether our 'best' guess was an unbiased estimator or not. The absence of both actuarial and non-actuarial risks are required for perfect foresight (see Table 4.1).

Table 4.1 Risk and uncertainty

	Presence of actuarial risks	Absence of actuarial risks
Presence of non-actuarial risks	uncertainty and risk	uncertainty only
Absence of non-actuarial risk	risk only	complete certainty or perfect foresight

Repeated risk occurrences are of little consequence even to a risk-averse firm because the average outcome will always tend towards the expected outcome. However, when a firm confronts a single (or limited) instance(s) of risk, then its cost to the firm is as great as in an uncertain situation for there is no average outcome in only a single one (Knight [1921], 1946, 26–7). Firms will desire to minimise both uncertainty and single instance risk when contemplating either a production or investment decision. It may be possible to hedge or insure against the actuarial outcomes firms meet infrequently, such as fire, theft or interest rate movements, if a third party carries the risks of enough firms so that the average conforms to the expected outcome. However, it is not possible to directly hedge against non-actuarial risks such as the behaviour of competitors or political decisions.[5]

Uncertainty and the heterogeneity of economic situations primarily stem from human behaviour. Two separate contributing factors are involved. First, the existence of individual human creativity results in an unlimited number of possible situation–decision–action sequences. Secondly, since the results of some human decisions, such as the acquisition of formal technical knowledge, naturally accumulate, a given situation or the individual's perception of a situation *cannot* repeat itself. We cannot un-know what we have learned. Learning can be a two-edged sword. Learning which subsequently changes the decision-making parameters can increase firms' uncertainty, while learning about the shape and position of the *stable* decision-making parameters can reduce their uncertainty.

In the first learning situation, an individual may use knowledge acquired via learning-by-doing to imagine new opportunities or alternative behavioural sequences not hitherto thought of. New competitors, products or inputs may emerge which may affect the firm's input and output markets. Firms will be continually striving for another way to approach a given problem and the knowledge that this is occurring, inhibits others from believing that the same decisions will be made by other firms when similar situations occur. This hysteresis of decision and actions may be permanent, in the case of technical knowledge, or long term, in the case of tangible capital. On the other hand, learning others' behavioural patterns can be used to more accurately predict outcomes of given actions and subsequently lead to a more certain and determinate outcome for all parties provided these patterns are themselves steady and the costs of learning negligible. Repeated situations occur only when stable behaviour functions or objective natural phenomena dominate the decision functions. Generally, this applies to the classic price–quantity decision when learning does not influence the choice parameters but will not apply to once-off irreversible decisions such as the investment decision.

In contrast with behavioural patterns, most fundamental natural occurrences, such as those which arise from physics and biology, are usually either certain[6] or subject to actuarial variation. Firms can therefore, predict many aspects of the weather, particle behaviour and human health with a stable level of stochastic error. A few natural phenomena such as earthquakes and the discovery of new resources remain uncertain, but being rare, these do not dominate economic decision making (Pesaran 1987, 276–9).

While most of the relevant parameters for economic decision making are the outcomes of past decisions, many, of course, can be taken as given within more immediate time periods. Stocks of capital assets, the size of particular labour markets and the structure of industry can take considerable time to change not only because of the gestation time in their 'production' but because of the time people require to change their patterns of behaviour. We expect, therefore, that uncertainty will be greater when we speculate about more distant time periods.

Theoretical treatment of uncertainty

Uncertainty, arising as it does from unique non-repeated situations, applies particularly to the investment decision. For the firm, investments are most often irreversible and the objective forces that produce investment opportunities come and go and do not usually repeat themselves. When we consider in addition that each firm's perspective and judgement of a situation depends on its unique history and recent experiences, then the assessment of the investment situation is even more unique.

Knight and Keynes argued that when this form of uncertainty exists, firms cannot base a decision on an expected value calculated from a stable probability distribution function based on a finite set of events. A probability distribution function of possible outcomes cannot be constructed because there is not a list of exhaustive outcomes. Where objective constraints are limited, a conjectural infinite regress may preclude a determinate solution or range of solutions (Pesaran 1987, 276–9).

As a reasonable alternative to mathematical calculation, Keynes believed that rational firms will rely on conventions and rules of thumb. In practice this may amount to assuming that present circumstances will continue into the future, not because they believe this is probable, but because there is no reason, on balance, why it should change in one direction and not another.[7] We base our estimates of the future states of the world on what we know for certain rather than highly speculative prophecies that we hold with little confidence. Firms also look for behavioural patterns and changes to these patterns (Pesaran 1987, Ch. 2). This task is not fruitless. People seek regularity and a level of certainty in their lives by adhering to customs and conventions and these develop into behavioural patterns. Torr contends that we only require that people *believe* that there is an underlying regularity to the way others make decisions for regularities to develop (Torr 1988, Ch. 2). While we cannot predict behavioural content (that is, which product a person will choose) claimed Knight ([1924], 1935, 137), we have more confidence in predictions of form (that is, whether they will seek to buy more or less). What people are likely to do is an empirical question he believes. There are limits to the formal methods of science but it is possible to make generalisations (Knight [1924], 1935, 121–4).

This empirical approach to strategic or behavioural uncertainty has been adopted by management theorists who use empirical data to categorise firms according to identified strategic patterns (see McGee and Thomas 1988). However, as recognised by Marshall, Keynes and Rothschild, business customs and conventions are themselves dominated by fashion. Strategies are not necessarily grounded in objective forces. If everyone seeks to select the average type competitive behaviour, neither too far ahead or too far behind the pack, then the old infinite regress theories of behaviour reappear.[8] Like a herd of sheep on the move, the course followed can be unpredictable.

The game theoretic approach to the investment decision is not consistent with the underlying method of the Austrian or process competition theories adopted within this book, and cannot be used to determine the outcome under non-repeated situation uncertainty. Under process competition, the unique experience of members of each firm shapes their world view and the way they assess the profitability of given situations. Personal experiences dominate collective or statistical knowledge (Matthews 1991, 115–6). When firms hold divergent views, it is difficult for one firm to know how another firm will reason and respond to a given set of circumstances. Not only may firms regarding the same situation perceive different opportunities, but also they recognise that their assessment of the situation will not necessarily be shared by others. In fact what makes people entrepreneurs is the very confidence they have in their own ability to recognise missed opportunities . Accordingly, what is a rational response by one party to a situation is not necessarily rational to another party. A firm's conjecture about their rivals' rational responses to a given situation is limited by the firm's confidence in their perception of the way rivals reason and the facts rivals have at their disposal.

If one also considers non-economic behavioural motives (which since Mill [1836], 1984, 52–4, and J.N. Keynes [1917], 1984, 77) economists have ignored as an analytical abstraction only),[9] then the more conjectural iterations a firms goes through in order to guess/estimate how its competitors will respond, the greater is the degree of uncertainty. A firm may have some idea how a normal profit-seeking firm should behave but it cannot hope to know which social and political ambitions entrepreneurs and managers may harbour. If an inexplicable and unpredictable error creeps in to each layer of logical-time decision making, then the error will grow geometrically and convoluted decision making strategies will hold little predictive value.[10]

In non-game theoretic models of imperfect competition, the firm is represented either as a group-interdependent or as a quasi-monopoly firm. In the first version, the interdependent group operates under the protection of common market barriers and conjectures about other group members' reactions dominate decision making. The outcome will determine the group's rate of profit. This model is conventionally used to analyse the price-quantity decision in the context of uncertainty over rival decision-making behaviour. It takes little notice of investment, entry and possible defensive moves by firms to neutralise potential competition. Its treatment of uncertainty focuses exclusively on conjectural or reaction variation function models in the spirit of Cornet, Edgeworth and Bertrand. As such, it would appear to be more suited to oligopolistic markets, which are protected by apparently permanent exogenous barriers to entry.

In the second quasi-monopoly version, each firm behaves as if it operates within its own separate market (Robinson [1933], 1969, 52). There is a spectrum of competitors from close rivals to potential entrants and little coherent concept of the group. The rate of profit, which depends on each firm's superiority, due to efficiency or monopoly power, arises when the 'individual producer happens to be bounded on all sides by a marked gap in the chain of substitutes' (Robinson [1933], 1969, 5). Collusion between market incumbents is of secondary concern and implied demand schedules take as given, whatever rivals' reactions happen to be (*ibid.* 21). Uncertainty, which stems from the interdependence between rival firms, customers and suppliers, is broader than the conjectural uncertainty model and is dealt with in an entirely different way. It marginalises but does not ignore the price–quantity decision and an *ex ante* price–quantity decision is embedded in each investment decision. This model is more relevant when the central issues are investment and endogenous entry barriers. We do not use an explicit model in this chapter but this version is more relevant for our purposes and is a useful apparatus to keep in the background.

Uncertainty and project evaluation

The postulate of profit maximisation implies that investment will proceed when the present value of a project, appropriately discounted, is greater than or equal to zero. In the proposed scheme described below, we put aside the risk of default associated with progressively larger and larger borrowings of finance and assume that uncertainty is only associated with uncertain future events. Furthermore, to exclude unnecessary complications, we also exclude indivisibilities associated with the investment and production process.

In the presence of uncertainty firms cannot select an optimal profit maximising strategy based on an exhaustive probability distribution function of world states multiplied by the value of outcomes. According to Shackle ([1942], 1990, [1943], 1990, 53, [1956], 1990), to assume that we can possibly think of all possible outcomes (states of the world) is highly unlikely in business, for it is not uncommon for happenings to occur which surprise us because we had not thought of the possibility before. The more you think about what may possibly occur, the more you realise that the list of possible outcomes is infinite. Even if we can assign a probability to the possibility that an unthought of event will occur, if the event is unthought of, there is no way we can estimate a value for the outcome. According to Knight ([1921], 1946, 225–6) and Keynes (1937, 212–14), many events are so singular that even were we to give them a (subjective) probability, we may place such little confidence on that figure that it would be some how ridiculous to include it in our calculations.

Suppose that for each conceivable investment project, or what Shackle calls an action-strategy, the firm distinguishes between future states of the world as being credible or non-credible. Underlying each state of the world is the firm's belief about how rivals and customers will behave, both in response to the situation as it stands and in response to the proposed action by the firm in question. As the firm projects further and further into the distance, the scope of credible imagined states of the world grows, as time permits more changes due to a greater number and combination of reasonable behavioural sequences.[11] For near future forecasts, we assume Keynes's generalisation that firms form expectations on the basis that rivals, customers and other relevant parties continue to follow the same patterns and conventions of behaviour as they have previously held. In particular, rivals follow the same form of competitive and controlling strategies unless there are grounds for believing that a particular new direction will be adopted.

Where each credible state of the world is transformed into a profit per period P_j, we expect the dispersion of credible outcomes to increase with the length of the forecast horizon, as depicted in Figure 4.1. If firms are risk-averse, a higher dispersion of anticipated profit flows will cause the firm to hold the expected value of the profit flow per period with a lower degree of confidence or higher degree of uncertainty, than would have been otherwise.

In the less credible range of states of the world lie the non-exhaustive group of events which firms may only partly conceive of and over which they hold vague and unspecified degrees of confidence. If we suddenly imagine a new possible state of the world, it will affect the confidence of our profit flow estimates only to the extent that it changes the variance of the credible states of the world. It could lie outside the credible range and thus have no effect, or it could lie inside the range but reduce the variance of possible scenarios within each time period(s).

The unweighted mean value of profits[12] from the credible range in each period, $P^e = (1/n)\sum_{j=1}^{n} P_j$, is used to calculate a present value of profits

$$PV_\pi = \sum_{t=1}^{\infty} \frac{P^e}{(1+\pi)^t} \qquad (4.1)$$

Where

$PV_\pi =$ is the present value of profits, gross of depreciation
$P^e =$ expected profits, gross of depreciation
$\pi =$ the gross rate of discount $= i+x+\delta$
$i =$ the default free rate of interest set by the central bank
$x =$ the premium for uncertainty
$\delta =$ the depreciation rate.

The degree of the firm's tolerance toward uncertainty (y) multiplied by the perceived level uninsured-single-instance risk and uncertainty (U), determines x, the discount for risk.[13] Accordingly, the present value of profits for each investment project will rise as the firm's desire to tolerate profit estimates over which it has successively less confidence and more uncertainty rises (see Figure 4.2).[14] Similar curves can be drawn for other proposed action-strategies (investment decisions). Assuming the parameter that determines the relationship between the degree of confidence and the variance of credible outcomes is constant, then the slope of each line is determined by the dispersion of imagined credible states.

Figure 4.1 Dispersion of credible outcomes by investment time horizon

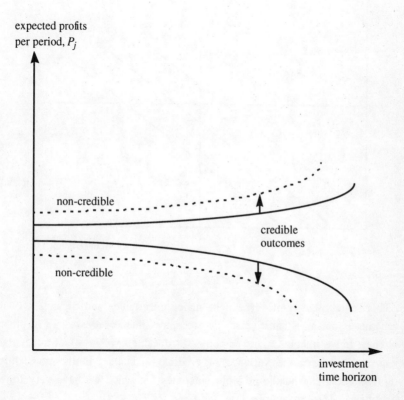

Each firm's own subjective tolerance to uncertainty determines the level of confidence with which it is prepared to operate. At a specific level of confidence as measured by the tolerated dispersion y^*, the firm will be expected to invest in all those projects which it supposes will yield a positive expected present value (provided of course there is unlimited investment funding) at the implied x. A rise in uninsured-single-instance-risk and uncertainty U will be expressed as an increased dispersion of credible outcomes and a flattening of the curves in Figure 4.2.

*Figure 4.2 Present value evaluations of investment projects according to
firm's tolerance of uncertainty and risk*

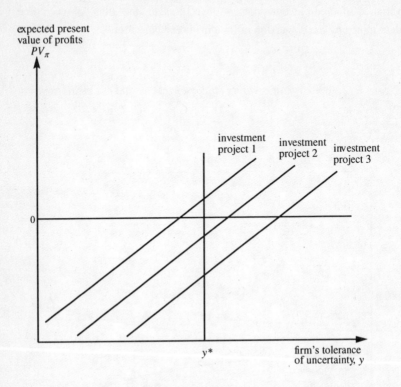

*Figure 4.2 Present value evaluations of investment projects according to
firm's tolerance of uncertainty and risk*

This representation of investment under uncertainty and Shackle's own scheme, is not an exhaustive set of outcomes situation dressed up in other clothes. If we imagine more outcomes, it doesn't have to affect either the expected value or the variance of credible outcomes. Furthermore, this representation can handle possible outcomes for which we have very little confidence. They are simply 'less credible'.

Containing risk and uncertainty

We assume that firms' desire to reduce their own uninsured-single-instance risk and uncertainty to improve the profitability of their choice to invest or not invest, and subsequently between one investment project and another. If the estimated costs of controlling the dispersion of credible outcomes outweighs the expected benefits, firms will only increase their knowledge in order to discover more accurately whether there exists a relationship between the current situation and future situations, and the form of this relationship. It may do this by undertaking market research and feasibility studies, economic forecasts and by gaining greater knowledge of government policy.

In situations where theoretical conjecture is ambiguous or lacking foundation, firms may respond to uncertainty by groping and feeling their way by a series of small steps toward what they feel is, on balance, the desired position, rather than by quickly moving towards it (for by definition it is possible to get enough information to estimate a closed probability density function in risk situations). Exploratory investment projects may be undertaken in order to test the market or the production process and reduce their uncertainty. These investments may provide the basis for changing production levels, product design, process technology and design, distribution and marketing, the target markets or the source and quality of inputs. The degree of uncertainty becomes a natural boundary to the level of investment expenditure along with the firm's general access to funds. This contrasts with the orthodox position that assumes that when faced with a sub-optimal position, firms make immediate and complete changes towards the optimal goal.

On the other hand, a firm which believes it is viable to control the dispersion of credible but uninsured-single-instance risk and uncertain outcomes, will ultimately seek to control human behaviour, the main source of uncertainty. These humans may be grouped as employees, customers, competitors and members of the government and their executives.

Employees
Firms desire to control both the work effort of employees and the quit rate of the valuable employees. The greater is the difference between the expected future employment remuneration of the employee's current firm and other firms, the less likely they will be to quit their current job. These anticipated advantages may include expectations of leave entitlements, superannuation, sheltered internal career ladders and superior wages. These measures come of course with a cost over and above the cost of offering these advantages. By linking its fortunes to a narrow group of workers, in particular by investing in their human capital, the firm is excluding potentially higher productivity workers (but of course reducing the possibility of employing a very low productivity worker). The threat of dismissal, as ever, remains an important device for controlling the work effort during working time. The firm may also devise an organisational structure, wage incentive scheme or system of industrial relations to ensure a more reliable and consistent work effort by employees. Unions and union leaders may be part of this scheme, especially

if the latter are susceptible to manipulation or bribery. In short, the firm invests in those goods that we have referred to as control goods.

Customers

Firms will also desire to develop a stable demand for their product by developing a product which is specifically targeted at a narrow segment of the market, by negotiating exclusive contracts with distributors and retailers and by using purchase contracts especially if they are intermediate suppliers. A captured customer market may be more certain but is possibly at the expense of a broader more lucrative market.

Competitors

According to Richardson ([1960], 1990, *xiv,*14), the need to control to some extent the investment decisions of potential or existing rivals in a market is necessary for investment to occur at all. If a large number of firms exist in a market, or entry is easy, a small variation in the average decision to increase productive capacity will have enormous implications for the total capacity in the whole market. Consequently, the dispersion of credible outcomes facing any given firm would be very wide indeed.

The best way to control the actions of rivals is simply not to have any. Firms may thus control the scope of competitors' behaviours by both increasing the economic distance between themselves and other firms and also by tacit collusion with those who remain close competitors. To achieve both these intermediate goals, the firm is required to invest in forms of endogenous market imperfections or barriers to entry. A firm builds up market barriers by making its intangible capital specific to a particular market and by exclusively focusing on its changing needs. This security is at the expense of the firm's ability to secure other markets, but it provides the firm with a more secure set of customers and reduces the number of competitors it must deal with and conjecture about. We discuss this process in the next chapter.

Mergers allow growth without inducing competition and may also raise the firm's market power and enable it to hurdle a market barrier.

Government personnel

Firms may also seek to limit the possibility of unpredictable decisions by members of a government (or indeed other external bodies such as competitors and suppliers) by tactics varying from gentle persuasion to bribes and blackmail. It will form and finance trade associations for this purpose.

The common thread throughout these measures is that firms invest in control capital in order to circumscribe their uncertainty.

Conclusion

To hold uncertain expectations over the outcome of a proposed action is normal because human behaviour makes most economic situations singular. More uninsured-single-instance risk and uncertainty tends to make investment plans more short-sighted and hesitant. Unless there are strong reasons for believing otherwise, firms will assume that current circumstances will continue on at least into the near future.

Where feasible we expect that a prudent firm, proposing to embark upon a scheme to raise the firm's productive capacity or to compete more actively with rivals, will also seek to invest in projects which improves its knowledge of possible investment outcomes and/or controls the scope of credible investment outcomes. One's judgement is improved by more knowledge. This may produce an incremental approach to investment, as the firm seeks to obtain knowledge over the market as it goes, or it may result in complementary investments in intangible control capital.

Notes

1. This list is not exhaustive. Lust, greed, envy and sloth are four of the seven deadly sins received as accepted wisdom by the early Christian Church.
2. The optimal or best guess price–quantity trade off will be already factored into the present values calculations for alternative investment projects. Hay and Morris (1991, 21) also describe the firm's objective function in terms of the investment variable.
3. Originally noted by Knight ([1921], 1946 especially 321) and Keynes (1937).
4. Shackle cited in Ford (1994, 82). According to Knight ([1921], 1946, 204) 'the presupposition of [actuarial] knowledge [is that] the world is made up of *things,* which, *under the same circumstances,* always *behave in the same way*' (emphasis in original).
5. One can sell an uncertainty to another party, but this merely transfers the uncertainty. It does not diminish it as in the case of actuarial risk.
6. Or as certain as is possible. No-one can be certain that the sun will rise tomorrow but aside from belief, this prediction is the most certain known to humankind.
7. Keynes (1937). Meeks (1991b) argues that this form of decision making is quite rational, in the sense of reasonable, in these circumstances.
8. Rothschild (1942, 120). Keynes ([1936], 1973, 158) argued that entrepreneurs and managers considered it better to fail conventionally than succeed unconventionally. Similarly, Loasby (1982, 127) asserts that entrepreneurs rely on excessive conformity in business strategies to provide the confidence necessary to make a decision. Spender (cited in McGee and Thomas (1988, 56) calls this borrowing strategic recipes from rivals. These views are supported by anecdotal evidence from the 1980s. Business fashions such as the importance of diversifying, going 'back to core business', lean production methods, just-in-time methods, the importance of merging, come and go. *The Economist* regularly cites business strategy rules of thumb, such as the 'four-to-one rule', in issue 22 April 1995, p. 30. Borner (1989, 83) even claims that over time the goals of multinational companies have altered. During the 1960s and 1970s, large corporations sought to maximise growth of sales revenue, but since then profit maximisation has received more prominence.
9. This may include the irrational aspect of competition referred to in Chapter 5.

[10] Also noted by Lavoie (1992, 51) game theory can only be applied when the list of possible outcomes are exhaustive.

[11] Each state of the world would be defined with respect to the firm's anticipations of the macroeconomy, cost and qualities of inputs, price and type of rival products, internal efficiency of the firm and other exogenous changes such as those arising from the government sector.

[12] This accords with Knight's ([1921], 1946, 222–4) view that when determining factors are inherently unknowable because of chance factors (not ignorance), they are equiprobable. We can always break up outcomes of differing probability into equi–probable portions. Non-equi-probable outcomes are due to the presence of a cause not chance factors.

[13] As discussed in Chapter 3, π represents the required rate of profit or the normal discount rate.

[14] The firm has the option of shutting down the project if negative profits eventuate.

5 Competition

Introduction

Without the presence of risk and uncertainty, the process of competition would not begin. Why would an average entrepreneur and capitalist go through the process of pitting one's wits against another, if outcomes concerning the preferences of consumers and suppliers and the decisions of rivals were known or calculable? If we know how fast our competitors will run, we will either aim to just out-pace them or we will just give up (if we cannot).

Most of the unknowns in establishing the profitability of investment arise from non-actuarial uncertainty. Outcome statistics of past and present business ventures, regardless of their scope, can only *guide* our predictions of the outcome of an individual case. An individual outcome will depend more on the talents and experience and insights of the particular management team operating an untested scheme in a novel environment. It depends on the specific behaviours and decisions which unique parties bring to bear on specific circumstances.

The process of competition is more than the decision to set price and production levels. It is an unfolding sequence of creating and destroying *endogenous* barriers to entry into specific markets. Endogenous barriers are temporary barriers which firms create by their own investment activities. These investments only create barrier assets if they give their firm at least a temporary advantage over potential entrants and nearest economic rivals. They may include knowledge investments such as the acquisition of better market information or the development of the ability to use this information to better advantage. Or it may include investment in control capital such as the accomplishment of successful research and development projects, novel efforts to reorganise and reform the workplace, superior access to distribution markets and more successful attempts to contain and control other market participants by rent-seeking activities.

These investments predominantly involve the creation of intangible capital. The acquisition of new plant and equipment which embodies the latest cost saving technologies, does not give the firm an advantage for long, as rivals can easily buy similar devices 'off-the-shelf'. Intangible advantages, though, are frequently harder to detect, understand and reverse engineer.

Endogenous market barriers give the firm some temporary ability to acquire above normal profits.[1] Barriers are more durable or lasting the greater is the cost or demand side advantage they impart to the firm and the less are rivals able to imitate or surpass them. Clearly not all attempts to create these barriers will be successful. The firm may find that even with these investments it just manages to maintain market share or achieve a normal profit. We argue below that endogenous barriers can only arise in the context of market uninsured-single-instance risk and uncertainty and it is because of this uncertainty that other firms' intangible advantages are so hard to duplicate or surpass. If perfect foresight or only actuarial and insurable risks exist, then competition will eliminate endogenous barriers as fast as they appear.

Exogenous market barriers on the other hand, refer to entry impediments caused by forces external to the firm. They remain in place because potential entrants do not believe it is economically viable to try to circumvent them by their own intangible investments. According to Kirzner (1973), these barriers usually only include government regulations or policies and monopoly ownership over unique and desirable inputs. Not all government regulations and monopolised inputs, however, give rise to exogenous market barriers. If it is possible by rent-seeking investment activities to change government policy, or if research and development activity can produce alternative inputs, these barriers are endogenous.

As we are portraying intangible investments as responses to the competitive environment, we are also accepting the method underlying *process* theories of competition rather than the conventional *static* theories. On this basis we briefly identify the two conceptions of competition. The following sections then discuss measures to define the intensity of process competition, the two sources of competitive fervour, the role of uncertainty in permitting endogenous market barriers and the way the process of competition is played out by firms.

Process and static competition

Competition is about rivalry and striving to excel, whether by fair means or foul. Its intensity will naturally fluctuate. A race may vary from a walk to a steroid assisted sprint according to the internal drive of the competitors. Almost by definition, competition involves a fallacy of composition. The *ex ante* sum of individuals' expectations of winning a race generally exceed unity, despite common knowledge on the abilities of other athletes and external track conditions. Without inconsistent expectations the race would have no entrants. It is the individual's confidence in him or herself not their willingness to play the chance factor that encourages them to enter the race.

Process (or Austrian) theories of competition emphasise ways firms compete and the subsequent effects this behaviour has for the ultimate purpose in hand, be it growth, innovation, welfare or efficiency. Competition is considered a disequilibrium activity which may drive the economy or industry to or away from or around an equilibrium position. On arrival at equilibrium – the ultimate position of complete dovetailing of plans and full knowledge of the objective data governing decision-taking – competition ceases.

By contrast the *static* or equilibrium theories of competition focus on the characteristics of the end point of competition. To the extent they are concerned with the process of attaining equilibrium, the analysis conventionally focuses on price variation. Competition under this static method serves the role of equating demand with supply in day-to-day markets by price adjustment, while the *process* method is concerned with the mechanics by which the rate of return on investment funds are equalised.[2]

The intensity of static competition is identified by an industry's location along the perfect competition–monopoly spectrum. At its most intense, competition is assumed to be so quick that processes are irrelevant (von Hayek [1946], 1949, 95-6), and at its least intense the firm is so lethargic that the process does not begin at all. Between these extremes where we might expect to find the process of competition emphasised, the convention within this school of thought has been to take industry 'imperfections' as data rather than as outcomes of competitive activity.[3] Net investment, according to these theories, depends solely on changes emanating from outside the economic system. The popularity of the static conceptualisation of competition possibly stems from the old and ongoing obsession within neoclassical economic theory with the determination of relative value and price rather than investment behaviour.

As a guide to understanding the entire range of firm behaviours under competitive pressure, the static theory of competition is clearly of limited usefulness. Even when our attention is focused on the behaviour of prices, the static equilibrium method is only appropriate when there exists a single equilibrium position with strong stabilising forces. Where the time taken to reach equilibrium is significant and/or where the presence of uncertainty or imperfect knowledge creates multiple, path dependent equilibria, then the ultimate resting point is of secondary interest to the path travelled.

Briefly, the defining characteristics of process competition are that

- competition is a sequence of events undertaken in historical (not logical) time, [4]
- decisions are not completely determined by objective economic forces but also depend on one's perception of those forces, human creativity and free expression. Perceptions are inherently heterogeneous between agents,
- decisions are taken within the context of uncertainty of the future and imperfect knowledge over present (and past) events. We cannot know whether *ex ante* cost and demand curves are unbiased estimates of the true functions, and
- objective demand and cost functions are transformed by the competitive process and are only data within any short term.

Imperfect knowledge and uncertainty imply that we cannot assume well-defined demand and cost functions upon which objective calculations can be made. As a result, not only will short-run demand curves be subjective and conjectural, but also long-run demand curves will be *highly* subjective and conjectural.[5] Thus the profit-maximising rule, marginal revenue equals marginal cost, is more of a tautology than a behavioural relationship. Consequently, the firm's mark-up on unit costs indicates what it believes about its own demand and marginal revenue functions, rather than what they are. In this context, firm behaviour is better described as profit-*seeking* rather than profit maximising.[6] Firms are still rational in the sense of making reasoned and purposeful decisions given available information and experience. Actions are not random or capricious. However, because there does not exist any mathematical or scientific basis for calculating the mean and variance of the profits of alternative actions, actions cannot be guided by *objective* optimal strategies, only expectational ones (Kirzner 1969, 1979, 166).

Defining intensity

Under the static notion of competition, the difference between price and marginal cost is conventionally accepted as indicating a firm's position along the monopoly–perfect competition spectrum. The literature on process competition, however, is less explicit about its definition of competitive intensity. The extent to which actions and investment by the firm are directed towards enhancing their cost and demand side advantages rather than just duplication of existing capacity, could serve as an indicator. These actions may include observed research and development activity, rent-seeking activities and actions to develop new markets and new products during any specified period.

If we abstract from changes to the conventional economic parameters, 'tastes and technology' (in the broad sense), more intensive profit-seeking efforts will lead to an equalisation of the rates of return between firms and markets as rivals vie to erode each others' market power. However, because our abstraction implies a fixed opportunity set, we would also expect the processes to peter out towards a stationary state *ceteris paribus*.

In many discussions of process competition, however, the development of innovations, new ideas and the generation of new consumer demands is endogenous to the competitive process. It is often less clear what the objective parameters are in this case, but limitations from science and innate consumer 'wants' are implicitly depicted as a spongy barrier which can be extended given time and resources. Accordingly, the actions of one firm pursuing an investment activity based on an imagined opportunity may be to the detriment of profits accruing to other firms in the economy. More intense competition thus leads to an increase in the dispersion of the rates of return between firms and there is no necessary reason why the process of competition will cease or lessen. Dispersal of the rates of return may be an indicator of more not less competition.

A large gap between price and the long-run marginal cost will reflect market power as measured by the current or anticipated availability of close substitutes in the product market.[7] However, compared with the static notion, the process view of competition provides no clear *a priori* reason why the presence of market power will be associated with fewer competitive processes. In fact we argue below that to the extent market barriers are endogenous to the firm's investment schedule, the presence of market power, albeit temporary, will be the result of more competitive manoeuvres.

In order to understand the variation in the intensity of process competition we have to accept that profits and greed are not the only force compelling the behaviour of the firms and the individual in the business of producing and selling. Even where profit-maximisation is a strong and systematic economic motive, it is not clear how we cope with situations where other aspirations dominate it in the hierarchy of human needs. We suggest that when there is a rise or fall in the business's perception of the threat of bankruptcy, this rearranges the ranking of motives so that to scour the market for every little opportunity becomes either more or less urgent. Unfortunately, it is not clear how this can be formally modelled without introducing complex multi-objective optimising functions.

As discussed in the preceding chapter, we argue that the effect of raising the urgency of greed in the ranking of human motive is to reduce the firm's aversion to uninsurable risk and uncertainty, that is, to increase its tolerance towards the risk and uncertainty associated with profit-seeking activities. This effectively reduces the x variable in the required rate of profit. Thus for the remainder of this chapter we will assume that the firm is a long-run profit maximiser subject to the proviso that the degree of competitive desperation is reflected in its aversion to risk and uncertainty and thus the (minimum) required rate of profit, π.

Sources of competitive pressure

Both changing prices and undertaking investments involve risk (especially in the light of rival responses) and, with regard to the latter, extra work. Pursuit of risk-bearing changes does not automatically occur as a result of a mere expansion or contraction of opportunity. Investment in knowledge may be required to 'discover' that demand, costs or technologies has changed or that opportunities exist in other markets. If it is satisfied with its level of profits or market share, it is quite plausible that a firm will not even undertake this preliminary investment.

A changing set of perceived opportunities for profits from either permanent or cyclical forces may facilitate business policy changes but cannot be responsible for initiating them. It takes some form of competitive pressure from within or without the firm to exploit these advantages. While the importance of competition is implied in almost all economic theory, it is often assumed to be so automatic that its course and intensity is beyond question. We argue here that a change to a firm's business practices can be sourced to either competitive pressures which originate from the collective behaviour in a market, or from the competitive and creative qualities of its workforce. We call the former external competitive pressures and the latter internal driving forces.

External competitive pressures
External competitive pressures arise from the number of rival firms producing close substitute products, combined with pressure from the variation of aggregate profits over the trade cycle. Clark's theory of 'workable competition' implies that the intensity of competition within a 'market' or 'industry' is determined by the internal competitive drive of its two most competitive firms. Competition is a sequence of aggressive and defensive moves and responses, which only a very small number of entrepreneurs in a market need undertake for competition to begin. Without

initial moves competition does not begin, and without defensive moves it does not spread (Clark 1961, 429).

We may extrapolate to argue that any exogenous changes, which alter the barriers between markets, will by changing the number of competitors, change the competitiveness of the market. An increase in the numbers of firms cannot reduce the internal drive of the two most aggressive firms but may increase it. A reduction of barriers may result not only in the merging of markets, especially between regions, but may also increase the entry of new competitors. Porter's large international study of competitiveness has suggested that active rather than potential entry is the crucial factor for determining rivalry. To enter, the firm has to have developed a specific market advantage and this development 'ups the ante' on incumbents (Porter 1990, Ch 3). Clark's workable competition thesis is consistent with industrial economists who attribute the rise in international competition since the 1970s to a reduction in tariff and non-tariff barriers and lower costs of transportation and communication.[8]

Falling aggregate profits may also exert a strong pressure on the firm to compete.[9] It can make competition a sink or swim affair.

A change in both forms of external circumstance affects the firm's perception that if it does not alter its current competitive behaviour, then the probability of ultimate bankruptcy will increase. It is the desire by equity holders to limit their numbers and maintain control over the firm that leads them to use debt rather than equity to finance the investment process. But it is the very presence of fixed debt commitments which makes the threat of bankruptcy more immediate and sensitive to current profits flows.

Internal competitive drive

Internal drive comes from the individual's personal qualities that have been nourished or suppressed by the broader cultural environment. Personal qualities express themselves as cunning (Marx ([1894], 1972, 253), alertness (Kirzner (1973, 9–11, 1976b, 123) or aggression (Clark 1961, 157). They are motivated by the desire for higher profits (Schumpeter, Marx), power and recognition (Knight, Schumpeter), the joy of creating (Marshall, Schumpeter) and the 'innate urge to activity' (Keynes, Scitovsky).[10] Creative and driven members of the firm create opportunities and do not just respond to opportunities that pass by. These internal urges can induce positive investment expenditure without recourse to the success or otherwise of past investments.

Motivations do not arise in a vacuum but are inhibited or promoted by cultural factors. According to Knight, there are no purely economic motives and the social situation furnishes much of the driving force behind competition.[11] These cultural forces include moral sentiments and sympathy for one's fellows (Smith, Marshall), inertia and resistance to change (Marshall, Schumpeter, Clark, Hayek, Eliasson, Best), intolerance to deviant conduct (Schumpeter, Clark, Ioannides), consumer alertness and attitudes (Clark), the competitiveness and professionalism of the business community (Clark, Auerbach) and entrepreneurs' experience and confidence (Kirzner).[12] Motivations are sustained according to Knight by a high interest in the game and this depends on a degree of unpredictability of the outcome, a comparability of players' abilities and the number and size of prizes.[13]

According to Kirzner, the existence of opportunity does not mean it will be perceived or embraced but instead depends on the 'alertness' of the entrepreneur.[14] Many innovations are considered obvious in retrospect. Some authors argue that a vast quantity of potential discoveries exist within the current set of known objective facts. Actual discovery depends on the ability of individuals to synergise by recombining knowledge.[15]

While a moderate level of external competitive pressure force firms to keep up with the average level of efficiency or the market power of their rivals, more dire external pressure and internal driving forces are expressed as the need to pull ahead of the crowd and win. Subjection to moderate external pressure may only force firms to adopt those ways of doing business and innovations, which are generally, considered industry standards. State-of-the-art cost-minimising and demand-bolstering measures are virtually purchased off-the-shelf from a well-established investment goods industry. By contrast, the entrepreneur's need to excel and inner confidence will be expressed as his or her desire to raise monopoly profits by developing endogenous market barriers. These barriers involve the investment in heterogeneous intangible capital which are unique in some respect and not bought ready-made.[16] A higher degree of external pressure raises the probability of ultimate bankruptcy if the firm does not alter its current competitive behaviour. The more desperate is the firm, the greater its tolerance towards the uncertainty of investment and therefore the lower is x and π.

Uncertainty and market power

This section represents a minor diversion from the main thread of this chapter. It investigates whether endogenous market barriers are possible or whether they will be automatically eliminated by competition. We suggest here that uncertainty of the investment decision, especially for intangible goods, is the critical feature, which allows the firm to acquire some level of endogenous market power, and thus produces Robinson's 'world of monopolies' (Robinson, [1933], 1969, Ch. 27). Specifically, it is *other* firms' uncertainty of future changes that encourages the evolution of heterogeneous intangible capital that thus permits a particular firm to earn endogenous monopoly profits.[17] Uncertainty causes sunk costs and irreversibilities that penalise an inappropriate choice.

Under conditions of complete certainty by all agents and in the absence of exogenous barriers to entry and indivisibilities of the production process, only a normal rate of return will accrue over both the short and long run.[18] Furthermore, in situations of repeated actuarial risk or insurable risk, the rate of profit will be normal, for the average outcomes of these risks tends asymptotically to the expected value and the cost of the risk *per se* (but not necessarily the actual event which is reflected in insurance costs) to the firm is negligible. Single (or limited instance) actuarial risks, which for some reason are not insurable, are uncertain risks from the firm's point of view, and should be classified as part of uncertainty.

Unless the firm has complete certainty over both the production process – that is, the reliability of turning inputs into output – and the market valuation of the product, investment and production involve, at some level, sunk costs. Sunk costs comprise expenditure or benefits forgone that may not be recouped in the form of future benefits. The degree of sunk costs hinges on the level of uncertainty in both the firm's internal operations and external markets. The more uncertainty there is, the greater is our misjudgement about events and the greater are the losses we may sustain. From the firm's perspective, if it had complete certainty, if every product was custom made and if price was contingent on the costs of production there would be no room for sunk costs.

For our example, assume that exogenous barriers to entry do not exist. Consider the situation in which either the static perfect competition or the dynamic perfect foresight apply. A particularly large number of investment projects, which yield the maximum rate of return, will exist. The firm's vision, under these circumstances, will not be limited to its home market. It knows with certainty all future parameter changes in all other markets far in advance of the said changes. Hence any 'barrier' to operating successfully in a market due to the need to develop technical skills, organise large and complex systems of production or develop market networks and distribution systems can be planned well in advance and with complete certainty that they will be profitable.

Perfect foresight means, however, that all other firms can invade the firm's own home market without risk and with perfect timing and the occurrence of above normal returns in any market is instantaneously eradicated. The Marginal Efficiency of Capital (MEC) schedule is horizontal with respect to the level of investment expenditure by the firm during a time period. With complete certainty, which must include the knowledge of rival firms' market entry decision, endogenous market 'barriers' are fixed costs but they do not receive an above normal return. There are no extra costs of entering new markets and there is no systematic reason why investment projects in one's home market should be more profitable than those in far-flung markets. All firms choose the same optimal investment strategy and production process and capital is accordingly homogenous.

Under *imperfect* certainty however, different potential investment opportunities appear to offer different prospective rates of return, because the knowledge and understanding of markets and processes with which the firm is familiar gives it a cost or demand advantage over other firms. Thus the firm does not believe that any above normal returns will be immediately eradicated by other firms' competitive behaviour. Each firm will rank prospective investment projects according to their anticipated rate of return and the MEC will slope downwards as indicated in Figure 5.1. A change in the business climate (perhaps due to changes in the trade cycle), the level of optimism or stability of the economic environment will raise the level of confidence associated with any investment project, *ceteris paribus,* and will raise the MEC schedule in Figure 5.1.

The firm who follows a successful investment course will earn above normal profits for as long as it takes rivals to recognise their excessive profits, understand why and how they have been successful and to copy them. This process can take considerable time, especially if the original firm is successfully evolving further ahead.

We have used complete certainty as an unrealistic abstraction to illustrate how important the presence of uncertainty is for explaining endogenously created imperfect competition and market power. There is no implication that certainty exists. Uncertainty is an inherent feature of economic processes where decisions are continually being made in the context of a unique environment and the range of possible outcomes are not objectively quantifiable and are non-exhaustive.

Figure 5.1 Ex ante *investment rate of rate of return for the firm according to its perception of uncertainty*

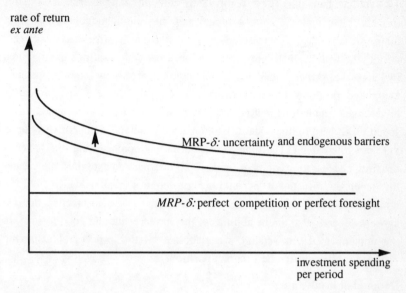

rate of return
ex ante

MRP-δ: uncertainty and endogenous barriers

MRP-δ: perfect competition or perfect foresight

investment spending
per period

The process of competition

If firms are motivated or compelled to compete or to compete harder than before, there are several basic routes they may take. They may reduce price. However, if their rivals are simultaneously developing cost-saving process technologies or new products and marketing devices, then a single price reduction will only be of short-term benefit. It may result in a Pyrrhic victory if large fixed costs exist, such as debt outlays. A successful and financially stable rival will ultimately be able to undercut the firm in subsequent periods using their new innovations. It is threatened obsolescence, not price competition that compels the firm to compete (Best 1990, 120). Accordingly, if firms are long-run not short-run profit maximisers, price variation will be a minor part of firms' competitive strategy. Findings from industrial economics generally support the view that firms are long-run profit maximisers (Hay and Morris 1991, 16, 296).

Firms may also seek to compete by merger, which enables them to raise their efficiency by gaining economies of scale, or bolster their price by acquiring market power. Again, if we accept evidence from the industrial economics literature, the evidence for these motives is weak. Instead, it appears that firms usually engage in mergers to pre-empt their own acquisition or to buy pre-made intangible control capital.[19] Waves of mergers come and go as a fashion and they are not conventional tools for competition.

It remains then that firms compete by undertaking specific investments (hopefully) to increase control capital and thus either monopoly power or their cost advantage. For these advantages to last at least beyond the current period, the firm needs to prevent imitation. Intangible control capital, which includes the skilled work team, the culture of the workplace, patents, negotiated positions within industry and market networks and protective government regulations, by its very nature tends to be heterogeneous, firm-specific and hard to duplicate. It is often a more suitable competitive weapon than tangible capital. The more driven is the entrepreneur, and the better is the firm's access to investment funds (both internal and external), the greater the level of investment expenditure on control capital which will be undertaken during any given period. However, success in erecting durable barriers depends also on the abilities of the entrepreneur and good fortune. In the remainder of this section, we elaborate on this process of achieving endogenous barriers to one's market position.

Demand-side advantage

Demand-side control capital or barriers relate to the availability of substitute goods in terms of the type and quality of the good, its correspondence to market demands and/or its accessibility to consumers. Because of changing market needs and the leapfrogging innovation process, many barriers stem from the firm's *ability* to innovate and adapt rather that its exclusive possession of a single idea or patent.

Large capital requirements for an industry, due perhaps to a high minimum efficiency scale (MES) threshold, does not on its own constitute a barrier to entry.[20] The share market, partnership and joint venture provisions, and equity trust institutions enable rentiers with small amounts of capital funds to combine to form a large company if rates of return are most attractive in industries with high MES. The fact that large companies are rarely started from scratch this way[21] does not suggest a lack of appropriate financial instruments, but rather the operation of other factors, such as uncertainty and the absence of relevant knowledge and control capital.[22]

Similarly, the existence of product differentiation and advertising does not on its own imply that goods are distant substitutes or that the goods cannot be copied easily or replaced in the market by superior goods. As is well recognised, product innovation and advertising may be facilitators for entry. Many firms will only seek to enter a market if they have a new product which gives them an advantage over established firms, and they use advertising to offset consumers' information costs. The need to offer a wide variety of brands and complementary products as a prerequisite to entry can be a form of large capital requirements barrier. As such, it fails to be a barrier on its own for the same reason given above. Both large-scale capital requirements and product differentiation constitute barriers only to the extent that it takes a knowledgeable and skilled competitor *time* to organise an equivalent organisation or demand for their product.

Demsetz has implied that the heterogeneous and firm-specific nature of intangible capital is the only valid source of endogenous barriers (not his terminology).[23] We extend this argument to suggest that without uncertainty there is no reason why only a small number of firms would have discovered the extra profitable nature of a particular barrier. This heterogeneous capital distinguishes one firm's product from its competitors according to design, technical characteristics, proximity to customers' needs, and physical and temporal access to customers. The extent to which endogenous capital cannot be imitated and or superseded by rivals (and to some extent reproduced by the firm itself), determines how inelastic and unyielding a barrier is. The longer the time it takes a potential competitor to surmount a barrier, the more likely there will be fewer close competitors and the greater is the possibility of above normal returns.

Not all intangible control capital is of the kind which gives a firm market power advantage. Many intangible investments are mere applications of known and tested ways to market products, distribute products, retrain the labour force, reorganise the workplace and/or solve industrial difficulties. To the extent these new ways are generally known and easy to acquire, a firm will be forced to consider implementing them as part of the competitive compulsion to earn normal profits and keep up with rivals, or as a natural way to increase the productive capacity of the business rather than as part of its drive to seek monopoly profits by creating a barrier to entry.

Cost-side advantage

A cost-side control asset or advantage may be expressed as enhanced firm efficiency and cost advantage. To prevent the owner of the cost-saving asset claiming any advantage as rent, the firm will endeavour to make its value firm-specific. Thus the asset owner cannot use competition for the asset to extract a price on a par with its current value to the firm.[24] Similarly, it is also in the interests of firms to make the character of the products as difficult to imitate or surpass by rivals as it can (and thus keep the long-term price elasticity of demand low) so they can extract as much market power as possible.

Emulation

The ease with which rival firms can imitate or supersede other firms' advantages or their economic distance relates to the comparative efficiency and market power between rivals. We argue here that much (intangible) control and knowledge capital may be inherently time-intensive to accumulate relative to tangible capital because the rate at which people can change their behaviour, change their understanding and change their desires is slow. It takes time to change consumer preferences, to develop complex and extensive distribution networks, to train and educate the labour force, to change government regulations, to change the culture of a workplace and generally acquire the knowledge necessary to produce and market a profitable product. This may account for why case studies show that early movers often sustain their advantages (see Porter 1990, Ch. 2). While investing more funds into changing these attitudes and behaviours may produce faster responses, we expect that the human condition imposes limits on the acceleration of change.

The firm maximises monopoly profits by developing firm-specific capital which is in some measure unique and differentiable from other firms' capital (Gilbert 1989). Generally, firm-specific capital can only be produced by the firm's own novel and innovative steps, whether through learning-by-doing or a deliberate intangible investment decision. Heterogeneous capital cannot be bought as a standardised product from suppliers of capital. It must be painstakingly searched out by trial and error and implemented in an often hostile and resistant environment. According to Nelson and Winter, replication of a sophisticated firm is not just a process of following blueprints and buying homogenous inputs in an anonymous market. The firm needs to develop specific organisational routines, which can be difficult.[25] Similarly, management theorists have argued that *the* essential character of success is the distinctiveness of firms' capital, both tangible and intangible. The broader the combination of firm-specific advantages, the harder they are to imitate.[26] The firm sustains its entry barriers by continuously investing in heterogeneous control capital.

The more complex an intangible asset is, the longer and more complex the sequence of investments that are required to produce the asset. 'Large firm' capital, that associated with complex organisational structure (internal and external) and large complex production and distribution systems, is typically of this nature. This capital cannot be bought off the shelf (only sold on a second hand market). It cannot be produced quickly by custom order as very large-scale plant and equipment can. It takes many years of building up and investing, learning-by-doing, trial and error processes and luck, to create a successful large firm. The provision of investment funds (either from debt or equity) reflects the incremental nature of a successful accumulation of large-scale tangible and intangible capital. Uncertainty associated with investment and the process of changing the environment, makes it prudent to lend or to invest by a step-by-step process. Learning-by-doing, experience, success and access to finance evolve by an iterative process, which allows firms to build up their capital.

Barriers may arise also because the firm cannot duplicate itself and produce more of the 'valued' good within a specific time period. This may be due to limited managerial resources (Penrose effect), limited entrepreneurial capital (Kalecki's 'principle of increasing risk') or unwillingness to lose control of the firm by new share issues (Kalecki's 'control loss' effect) (Kalecki [1939], 1990, Ch 4). While Kalecki's principle of increasing risk factor limits the rate of expansion of an existing firm, it does not on its own limit aggregate investment expenditure because it is possible for rentiers to combine to form a new company.

However, the role of knowledge and control capital in creating enough market certainty and control to make doing business worthwhile suggests that creating a large new firm from scratch is severely curtailed. Large firms are not created quickly by large investors or combinations of small investors who desire to enter a profitable market with a large MES. Such action would be very risky due to the existence of uncertainty in the market and the absence of suitable knowledge and control based capital in the market.[27] It does not have a brand name or regular relationships with suppliers, distributors, and customers. It does not have an established organisational structure, industrial relations system or workplace culture. Nor does it have a core group of skilled technical workers who have established workplace procedures and commonly agreed knowledge about how to go about production.

Entry to a 'large firm' market occurs by a cautious smaller scale entry, perhaps by an incremental merger of smaller firms. Large firms seeking to move horizontally into a new market will often do so by merger (takeover or acquisition) with an existing smaller firm in the target market. The entering firm seeks to learn-by-doing, and gradually establish market power by investing in control capital. If the existence of this complex capital can only be created by building it up over an extended period of time, then it will be scarce to the extent that any firm following this process may go bankrupt and to the extent that the optimal heterogeneous combination of knowledge and control capital shifts over time. Given this, 'large firm' capital barriers are more difficult to hurdle and we expect that large firms face lower demand elasticities and have the potential to earn higher rates of return on equity funds *ceteris paribus.*[28]

With respect to our discussion about barriers to entry above, the barrier to entering a market dominated by large MES technologies resides not in the financial impediment to combining the required level of equity, but to the uncertainty associated with creating the complex structure of (mainly) intangible capital to successfully run such a firm.

Conclusion

Firms compete by investing in heterogeneous intangible capital which gives rise to endogenous market barriers, unless they are operating under a very short profit horizon. The larger their capacity capital, and thus sunk costs, the greater the incentive they have to invest in complementary control capital. The latter is created by difficult to emulate demand- and cost-side market advantages.

Firms will search more vigorously for opportunities the more driven they are to compete. There is no reason why all possible opportunities will be known and already fully exploited, or why the most profitable investments will be undertaken first. Most investments, especially those which are firm-specific by design, are unique in some respect and the knowledge to confidently construct an objective probability density function of possible outcomes does not exist. Many opportunities cannot be known before other related investments are undertaken. Compared with standardised investments to merely keep abreast of competitors, investment activity designed to deliberately create heterogeneous, firm-specific intangible capital, will be subject to uncertainty, *a fortiori.*

The discovery of and investment in a profitable asset depends on the skill of the entrepreneur, his or her competitive drive and good luck. Under these circumstances, it is possible that specific endogenous barriers to entry are sustainable and do not immediately evaporate with 'normal' competitive behaviour. The tenacity of barriers depends on the firm's ability to conceal its successful attributes and the time it takes a rival to imitate or surpass them. The model of firm behaviour whereby it uses investment to maximise profits with an implied price–quantity decision, imparts more understanding for our purposes than the model of price–quantity setting to maximise profits with an implied investment decision.

Notes

[1] Or more correctly, a capital gain.

2 Knight ([1924], 1935, 107) contends that one limitation of applying scientific principles to economics has been the dominant role given within the science to the outcomes of activities rather than processes.

3 Bain ([1956], 1965, 4, 15) varies in his treatment and in some places views research and development as competitive weapons (37–8, 122), Lipsey (1977, 265–77), Hirshleifer (1976, 307–10).

4 For logical coherence, writers adopting the process approach to competition also view the capital-intensity of production as a time process or roundaboutness and the stock of capital as a fund.

5 Long-run demand curves are more uncertain because of greater potential for endogenous and exogenous changes to the market.

6 Profit-seeking has been described by Nelson and Winter (1982, 29) as the tendency to erode rivals' quasi-rents, while profit-maximising assumes instantaneous equilibrium and optimisation. The former assumes uncertainty and the groping cumulative nature of evolutionary theories, while the latter obscures them. This view appears to be sympathetic to Kalecki ([1940], 1991, 60–1). See also Sawyer (1989).

7 A substitute must be defined as close with respect to its various characteristics including availability to consumers.

8 See Clifton (1977, 148), Auerbach (1988, 1–8, 38–9), Cantwell (1989, 12, Chs 4 and 5).

9 The effect of falling aggregate profits on competition has also been mentioned by Marx ([1894], 1972, 253) and Clark (1961, 56, Ch. 8).

10 Marx ([1887], 1961, 258–9, 264), Knight ([1923], 1935, 46), Schumpeter ([1911], 1934, 91–4, 131), Marshall ([1890], 1920, 87, 136), Keynes ([1936], 1973, 163), Scitovsky (1992, 31–3, 62).

11 Knight ([1922], 1935, 36, [1921], 1946, *xxxiv*, 1923, 46). See also Sawyer (1989).

12 Harcourt (1994, 24), Reid (1989, *xi*), Marshall ([1919], 1923, 518, 653), Clark (1961, Ch. 8, 487), von Hayek (1978, 189), Eliasson (1988, 43), Best (1990, 253), Schumpeter ([1911], 1934, 83–8), Ioannides (1992, Ch. 5), Clark (1961, 264), Auerbach (1988, 4, 38–9), Kirzner (1973, 36, 66, 227).

13 Knight ([1921], 1946, 53). See also Odagiri (1992, 15–18) who argues that the large difference in rewards for winners and losers in the Japanese ILMs enhances rivalry.

14 See Kirzner ([1969], 1979, 119, [1976a], 1979, 130).

15 Best, seminar Queens' College, University of Cambridge, May 1995.

16 Unless the firm is prepared to sacrifice profits it will eventually have to introduce the generally available innovations and new ways which its competitors have adopted. The presence of a barrier merely gives it more flexibility about when it introduces these investments.

17 In this respect we are similar to Knight ([1921], 1946, 34–5) who attributed abnormal or pure profits to the presence of uncertainty or ignorance of the future. Consequently, a firm will aim to reduce its own uncertainty and increase its rivals uncertainty.

18 Under normal profits however, capital have to be capable of duplication or emulation by a rival seeking to share in any monopoly profits which may exist. Thus there is some contradiction in claiming that a certainty based theory can accommodate heterogeneous capital. Complete divisibility of the production process eliminates natural monopolies.

19 See Hay and Morris (1991, Ch. 12).

20 Bain ([1956], 1965) and Clark (1961, 157, 298, 487, Ch. 8) give these as barriers.

21 Virtually all firms start as small businesses (Hay and Morris 1991, 276).

[22] As discussed in Chapter 8, the presence of Kalecki's lenders' and shareholders' risk also acts to limit the rate at which a firm can grow and thus expand into other markets, especial those requiring a large amounts of capital funds for entry.

[23] Demsetz (1982, 50–1). Marshall ([1919], 1923, 165) also thought that every manufacturer has some advantages over its rivals but they were not permanent and could be copied.

[24] It is also possible that special contracts enable firms to retain the use of capital at prices below their full value. This may occur in the labour market where the firm has paid for education or training or in the land rental market, where part of the land value is determined by the activities of the leasee and its neighbours rather than its location *per se*.

[25] Nelson and Winter (1982, 119). See also Doz and Prahalad (1988, 350), Kogut (1988).

[26] Harrington (1987), Pettigrew *at al* (1989), Ray *et al* (1989), Cantwell (1989, 18–19), Porter (1990, Ch. 2).

[27] The use of seed finance, that is, floating an entirely new company on the stock market, is rare. Most new floats are of existing unlisted companies.

[28] This does not mean that large firms will necessarily earn above normal profits. If a firm has to grow to a certain size before it can operate profitably, then the risk component x of the normal rate of profit will accordingly be higher than other markets, and it may appear that abnormal returns to equity are being made.

6 Empirical Evidence

Introduction

Several attempts have been made to measure the level and growth of intangible investment and capital in industrialised economies in recent years. Most of these studies aggregate expenditures on education, training, health and research and development across all sectors of the economy and find very high levels of intangible investment expenditure. According to recent estimates by Kendrick (1994, 1), intangible investment accounted for almost half of US GDP in 1990. Our empirical work, presented below, uses a narrower definition, which more closely parallels the conventional notion of gross fixed capital formation. We find smaller but faster growing levels of intangible capital and investment over the last half century.

Accounting for intangible capital and investment is important for the very same reasons that we regard fixed capital and investment as important.[1] Both forms of investment are a source of future productivity growth, to ignore a major part would be to bias statistical work and exclude potential explanatory factors. Both forms of investment are volatile components of expenditure and both forms of investment contribute toward and result from the trade cycle. In addition, both forms of investment are necessary for the health and future existence of a business.

Unlike earlier studies, which emphasised the household sector, we attempt in this chapter to limit our estimates to profit making firms. As such it is the intangible counterpart of gross fixed capital formation, one measure used by economists and policy makers as an index of growth and recession.

Several difficulties immediately present themselves when we try to measure either intangible investment or intangible capital. If we follow an expenditure approach, we find that like services in general, it is difficult to control for the considerable heterogeneity of the commodity and consequently derive price indices for constant levels of output. Furthermore, a lot of intangible capital will be produced by the firm for itself given the heterogeneous and firm-specific nature of the asset. On a more practical note, we find that cross-country data series on expenditures on research and development, workplace training, marketing and other forms of workplace investment are either very short, irregular or absent altogether. The OECD research and development data, which date from the early 1960s, appears to be the longest time series

55

but research and development is only one aspect of intangible investment.[2] Despite this, and because of its availability, this series has been the main focus of attention in the intangible measurement field.[3]

Because of these deficiencies, we have chosen two less conventional methods for estimating intangible capital and investment, and for practical reasons this has limited us to a single country. The first method calculates a capital stock series by using stock market records since the late 1940s to derive an implied level of intangible capital. The second method calculates an investment series from data on the portion of people who are working in a job which produces intangible investment goods, either for sale or for the internal use of their own firm. Both methods use data from Australia only. Australian stock market data, unlike many other countries, is highly suited for our ends because of the longstanding 'Generally Accepted Accounting Principle' to adjust asset values for inflation and fundamental factors.[4] Accordingly, the high level of inflation during the 1970s and 1980s should not unduly bias the series upwards. In fact we find no evidence that the series exhibits an upward bias arising from the escalation of prices between 1974 and 1990. We find instead that an abnormal drop in the aggregate profit share during the decade following 1974 actually led to a downward bias in our intangible capital series.

Stock market series

Accounting principles traditionally comply with economic notions of costs and benefits and until recently, most balance sheet data are records of the accumulation, depreciation and disposal of tangible capital items. In recent years, there has been some attempt to record intangible assets that confer value upon the company from the use of legal rights. These include patents, copyright trademarks, franchises and realised goodwill. However, our earlier discussion has argued that this is likely to be a small subset of all intangible capital. Our calculations estimate that total intangible capital was from three to four times greater than measured intangible capital in Australia between 1992 and 1997.[5]

Our interest in using stock market data arises, however, not from any regard it pays to intangible capital, but from the lack thereof. If we view the balance sheet as a record of tangible assets then, the balance of the value of a company must, by definition, be accounted for by intangible capital. Our estimates are derived from two company identities:

$$K_t + K_i \equiv K$$

and

$$ps + L \equiv K \ .$$

Where

K_t = present value of tangible capital.[6]

K_i = present value of intangible capital.

K = total present value of the company (= discounted value of future profit streams)

p = price of ordinary shares

s = number of equivalent ordinary shares on issue

L = value of liabilities.

Formal stock exchange records generally provide enough information to derive a measure of K_i/K for each company. The minimum data requirements include the share price, the number of shares on issue, and a measure of tangible capital and liabilities. Our time series is based upon data from publicly listed Australian companies between 1947 to 1998. The sample was based on a random selection of 20 per cent of firms listed in 1947 and 20 per cent of firms listed in 1997. The same firms were traced over time. Efforts were made to follow large companies that had been taken over or underwent a change of name. Given the high birth and death rate, the sample size fell during the intervening years and so an additional 7 per cent of firms, which were listed in 1971, were also included in the full sample. With the exception of 1986 to 1989 when liabilities had to be estimated, the sample size varies between 61 and 113. The sample during 1986 to 1989 constituted 42, predominantly larger, firms.

Price and share data was taken from September of each year (except October in 1989). September was chosen as a month least likely to include abnormal or seasonal price fluctuations. Each year, except 1986 to 1989, we were able to record information on price per ordinary share, number of equivalent ordinary shares on issue, a measures of net tangible assets (either net tangible assets per share or price per net tangible assets per share) and liabilities (current and long term).[7] Where variation in the presentation of prices occurred over time, the chosen price in most cases was the price that would bias the final series toward not finding a positive trend. Liabilities for 1986 to 1989 were estimated by linear extrapolation between 1985 and 1990. At time of writing, liabilities for 1998 were not available and 1997 values were used instead.

Depending on the available data series we estimate K_t and K_i as:

$$K_t = (NTAS)s + L$$

$$K_i = ps - (NTAS)s$$

$$K_i = ps - \left(\frac{p}{PNTAS}\right)s \ .$$

Where *NTAS* is net tangible assets per share and *PNTAS* is price per net tangible assets per share.

Figure 6.1 *Ratio of intangible capital to all capital, publicly listed companies, Australia, 1947 to 1998*

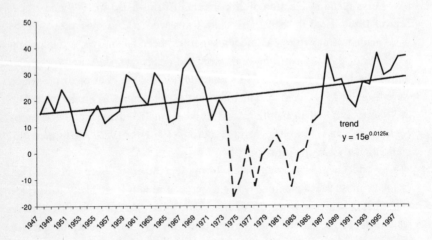

A graph of the ratio of intangible capital to total capital is presented in Figure 6.1. Stock market price data are a highly volatile series, which can often be dominated by irregular, seasonal and cyclical influences and is not surprising to see considerable variation in the line. Our interest, however, is only with the trend of this line.

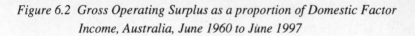

Figure 6.2 Gross Operating Surplus as a proportion of Domestic Factor Income, Australia, June 1960 to June 1997

1974 and 1984 stand out as an aberration from the rest of the data series. From 1975 to 1987, excluding 1980, Gross Operating Surplus as a proportion of Domestic Factor Income was considerably below other years between 1960 and 1997 (Figure 6.2). During this period, subdued profits were reflected in abnormally low real share prices. Accordingly we may justify our exclusion of this 10-year period as being an anomaly arising from an unusual combination of policy, institutional and overseas influences. Excluding these years, the proportion of intangible capital in listed companies grew at an annual rate of 1.25 per cent from 1947 to 1998. If we include the 1974 to 1984 period in our trend calculation, the average annual rate of increase in the proportion of intangible capital is reduced to 0.2 per cent. Under the higher estimate, intangible capital as a proportion of total capital has been rising by 2.5 percentage points every decade. Under the lower estimate, it increases by 1 percentage point.

The average share price divided by the NTA per share also exhibits a rising trend. This series which excludes liabilities, increased by 0.65 per cent per annum over the period 1947 to 1973 and 1985 to 1998 (see Figure 6.3).

As mentioned above, there is little evidence that the significant price rises experienced following the OPEC oil increases during 1973–74 and 1979 led to an overstatement of prices relative to firms' NTA and thus an overstatement of the proportion of intangible capital. The trend rise in intangible capital was evident before 1974 and has continued through the low inflation 1990s.

Figure 6.3 Share price over Net Tangible Asset per share, weighted average of listed companies, Australia, 1947 to 1998

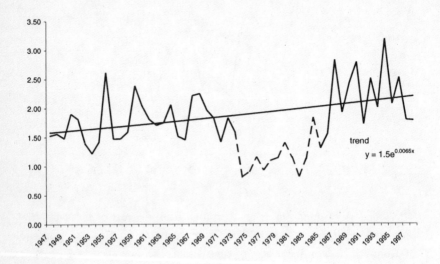

Employment series

The second estimation series uses the (international) principles underlying the definition of the conventional gross fixed (intangible) capital expenditures to create a parallel series for intangibles. Outlay and input–output table data from firms are not clear enough to enable us to derive an expenditure based series and the best we can do is to mimic this with an employment series. We shall define gross intangible capital expenditure to be outlays incurred by organisations (enterprises, general government bodies and private non-profit organisations) in acquiring intangible assets, whether these are purchased in the market or produced on own account. The purchasing firm may use these assets for their own profit or for the benefit of the general public. They include:

- Outlays associated with the development of intangible capital such as the skills, knowledge and useful talents of the workforce, market and technical knowledge, goodwill and brandnames, developed channels of access to markets, usable research and development and an efficient workplace.

- Outlays which significantly extends the productive lives of existing intangible assets.
- Work-in-progress.

Gross intangible capital expenditure does not include improvements to tangible buildings, constructions, plant and equipment. However, it does include byproducts of this process, improvements to the skills, knowledge and useful talents of a responsible workforce which arise from learning-by-doing. For example, the services of architects are not included because they are embodied in a tangible form, but the contribution their work makes to skill accumulation is.

While Gross Fixed Capital Expenditure excludes depreciation due to the use of tangible capital, our intangible counterpart includes appreciation associated with the use, application and refinement of intangible capital. Capital appreciation and in-house production are very much one and the same thing. Like services in general, where statisticians have difficulty defining a constant commodity, we also have difficulty in distinguishing between when intangible capital has improved or expanded. Unlike tangible capital, most intangible capital by its very nature is malleable and continuous.

For reasons discussed in Chapter 5, we expect that a large portion of intangible capital is produced in-house rather than bought from outside. Intangible capital tends to be more heterogeneous and firm-specific than tangible capital. When the nature of the work undertaken is non-standardised, informal and innovative, then a direct interactive mode of production is required. Before the 'American system' of interchangeable parts was invented in the 1850s, skilled tradespeople were required on-site to individually tailor and manufacture replacement parts (Best 1990, Ch 1). Personal contact was integral to production. In a similar vein Douglas ([1921], 1968, 18–19) wrote of the system of skill acquisition that '[w]henever a trade, craft or profession has developed to such a stage the general principles and scientific causation can be abstracted from personal contact, then apprenticeship . . . declines. That which was an art becomes a science with more or less fixed rules and generalized method of procedures'. The development of informal work skills and knowledge, brand names and distribution networks is still an art and thus still mainly produced in-house.

For reasons discussed by Marshall ([1890], 1920, 76–8), household expenditures are deemed consumption items even though many are undertaken with a view toward long term ends and benefits. Accordingly, we exclude the home production of education and welfare even though their contribution to societies' intangible capital is probably large.

Military sector production is also excluded for consistency with the measure of gross fixed capital expenditure.

Table 6.1 Production sectors

Production sector		
I. Organisations and enterprises	a. Private enterprises *	
	b. Public organisations	(i). Public Enterprises*
		(ii). Other (administration, defence, schools)
	c. Non-profit	(i). Schools, education
		(ii). Community, welfare
II. Households		

Note: * Indicates the for-profit sector

Enterprise gross intangible capital expenditure is the sub-section of the above which operates for profit. It excludes intangible investment expenditure produced by the non-profit government and organisation sectors. Only the intangible assets produced by private (I.a.) and public enterprises (I.b.(i).) are included (see Table 6.1). Our estimates of both total and enterprise gross intangible capital expenditure have been derived from historic census data on the distribution of employment according to whether the implied job contributes directly or indirectly to the growth of firms' intangible capital bases and whether they are produced by specialist investment firms for sale to end-using firms or whether they are produced within the using firm.

Employment data from the full enumeration of the Australian Bureau of Statistics Censuses of Population and Housing 1971, 1981, 1986, 1991 and 1996 is given in Table 6.2.

Five industry divisions are provided.

1. Firms involved in the direct production of research and development, advertising, marketing and promotion of production, the industry or the firm, workplace and financial reform and improvement for profit.
2. Other enterprises producing for profit.
3. Non-profit sector (government and other) involved in the production of education, training, data collection and dissemination.
4. Other non-profit sector establishments.

5.   Defence.

Occupations are classified into

1.   Those that directly produce products which embody intangible assets in other people or other intangible forms. These include teachers, trainers, sales and marketing workers, management consultants, research and development staff, financial advisors and people involved in the collection, retrieval and dissemination of information and knowledge.
2.   Those who as a byproduct of their work experience, acquire useful and relevant skills, knowledge and talents that contribute towards the goodwill, marketing and process efficiency of the enterprise or establishment.
3.   Other occupations.

Details of the industry and occupational classifications are provided in the appendix at the end of this chapter.

Table 6.2   Examples of occupations from the cross-classified employment data

Sector	Industry sector 1.	Industry sector 2.	Industry sector 3.	Industry sector 4.	Industry sector 5.
Occupation Sector 1.	A Marketing consult.	B Bank economist	C School teacher	D Gov't data processor	Military trainer
Occupation Sector 2.	E	F Industrial engineer	G University nurse	H Hospital surgeon	Army dentist
Occupation Sector 3.	I Unskilled worker	J Unskilled worker	K Unskilled worker	L Unskilled worker	Unskilled worker

Gross intangible capital employment includes all workers in occupations which are (mainly) dedicated to the production of intangible assets (A, B, C, D) and, in addition, workers in industries which mainly produce intangible assets (E, I, G, K) and a skill appreciation part of occupations whose work leads to significant learning-by-doing (F and H). The latter represents the rate at which work contributes toward the skills and other forms of intangible capital of the firm. Enterprise gross intangible capital employment includes only that part produced by enterprises (for profit), which are the first two industry sectors (A, E, I, B and a portion of F). Results from the census data are presented below in Figures 6.4 and 6.5.

Using our definitions, the proportion of the labour force involved in the direct production of intangible capital rose from 16.9 per cent in 1971 to 31.0 per cent in 1996 (Figure 6.4). The proportion of the labour force engaged in the direct production of *enterprise* intangible capital rose from 11.0 per cent in 1971 to 22.1 per cent in 1996. By contrast, there has been little clear trend in the proportion of the workforce who contribute toward intangible investment as a process of learning-by-doing. Over the last 25 years, the proportion of the labour force employed in the intangible capital sector, both enterprise and non-profit, has doubled.

These employment proportions would translate into exchange values if Australia was a completely vertically integrated economy and we weighted hours by wages. However, Australia is a small economy relatively dominated by the rural sector and it has a less complete manufacturing base than the US or EU. As such, we should regard these data as only indicative of trends elsewhere.

Figure 6.4 Proportion of employment in the direct production of intangible capital, Australia, 1971 to 1996

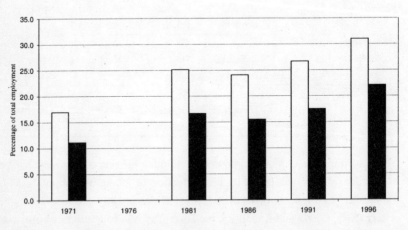

□ Occupations producing intangible capital (A, B, C, D, E, G, I, K) - all sectors
■ Occupations producing intangible capital (A, B, E, I) - enterprises

Figure 6.5 Proportion of employment in the indirect production of residual intangible capital (learning-by-doing), Australia, 1971 to 1996

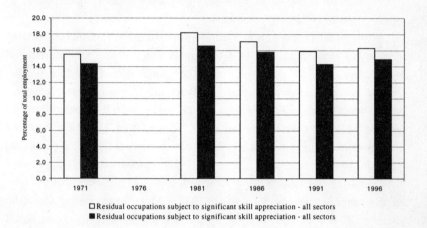

☐ Residual occupations subject to significant skill appreciation - all sectors
■ Residual occupations subject to significant skill appreciation - all sectors

Conclusion

In this chapter we have attempted to measure the level and growth rate of enterprise intangible capital and investment in Australia. These estimates are intended to be indicative rather than precise due to the difficulties of measurement. Calculations based upon stock market data find that intangible enterprise capital as a ratio of all enterprise capital has grown at an average annual rate of 1.3 per cent over the 50 years to 1998. Enterprise intangible investment as a ratio of all production rose by 2.8 per cent per annum in the 25 years to 1996 according to detailed employment data. The comparative (employment) growth rate for all intangible investment (including the not-for-profit and household sectors) was 2.5 per cent. If we convert these ratios to levels we get an annual rate of increase of enterprise capital of 4.0 per cent[8] and employment growth rates of 4.4 and 4.1 for the enterprise and all sectors respectively.

Our enterprise-based rates of growth are slightly higher than estimates made for the OECD. Deiaco *et. al.* (1990, 4) estimate that enterprise intangible investment within the seven largest OECD countries grew by 3.6 per cent per annum in the decade to 1984. This estimate excluded investment in training and organisational reform. Their ratio of intangible investment to GDP was 3.7 per cent in 1984 compared with our employment-based estimate of 15.5 in 1986. This difference arises because we have included intangible investment undertaken by firms for their own account. Expenditure based methods, such as those used by the OECD, are most likely restricted to investment products which have been openly transacted through the market. The difference is too large to arise solely from differing expenditure to employment ratios between sectors.

Published OECD research and development data indicate that in the two decades to 1996, research and development expenditure, both private and public, rose between 6.0 and 6.4 per cent per annum (OECD, 1979, 1997).

US studies on the level of intangible investment from all sectors, enterprise and non-profit, produce much higher levels but considerably smaller rates of growth than our estimates for Australia. Kendrick (1994, 3) calculated that all intangible investment as a ratio of GDP rose by only 0.5 per cent for the 60 years to 1990 and actually fell at an average annual rate of 0.2 per cent between 1973 and 1990. Similarly, Eisner (1989, 26) estimated that the ratio of all intangible investment activity to GDP fell by 0.3 per cent per annum in the 35 years to 1981. However, both Kendrick and Eisner's figures are based on real values of output, not employment levels as in the Australian case. Consequently, the US estimates are subject to the general difficulties associated with deriving price indices for services and heterogeneous commodities. Eisner believes that the deficiencies of his price indices probably led him to understate the 'true' level of growth of intangible investments. Furthermore, both Eisner and Kendrick include health expenditures, which we do not.

Finally, while the range of estimates given above provide a perspective of the size of intangible investment, it also highlights the need for a standardised definition for the purposes of future data collection.

Notes

[1] It is also an ambiguous and imperfect concept for the same reason that the concept of tangible capital is flawed. For example, as a present value concept it may depend on transient and inconsistent expectations. Further, since it cannot be defined independently from the definition of income, and income cannot be defined without a measure of 'intact capital', then conceptually capital involves circular reasoning (Hicks, [1946], 1986). Nevertheless, 'capital' does convey, in a practical sense, a measure of productivity and the roundaboutness of production.

[2] The OECD plan to release this series late in 1998.

[3] See, for example, Bos *et al* (1992).

[4] Asset revaluation has been 'strongly recommended' by Australian accounting bodies since 1978 (OECD 1980, 126). See also Barth and Clinch (1998), Cotter (1998).

[5] This estimate is based on our ratio of intangible to tangible capital to the respective ratios of 'other assets' to tangible capital for 1992 and 1997 for our sample of listed companies.

⁶ No distinction is made between the value of a company as a going concern and abnormal profits (as highlighted by Dimbath 1994) due to the overlap between them (as discussed in Chapter 5).

⁷ Liabilities were derived from the Official Record of the Stock Exchange of Melbourne, 1947 to 1971, The Australian Graduate School of Management, Centre of Research in Finance Annual Report Record Database 1951 to 1985, and Bloomberg on-line Historical data. Preference shares were not included as they were found in 1956 to increase tangible capital by less than one per cent. Similarly options were not included in the calculations unless they were part of the firms' NTA/Share calculation.

⁸ This is based on a trend rate of increase of aggregate expenditure of 3.7 per cent (From real expenditure on home produced non-inventory goods, Australia, September 1959 to December 1997, ABS AUSSTATS).

Appendix

Table A.1 Data for Figure 6.1

Year	Intangible capital/all capital (%)	Sample size	Year	Intangible capital/all capital (%)	Sample size
1947	15	76	1973	15	84
1948	22	69	1974	-17	82
1949	16	76	1975	-10	81
1950	24	80	1976	3	79
1951	19	79	1977	-13	83
1952	8	83	1978	-1	77
1953	7	82	1979	2	80
1954	14	79	1980	6	83
1955	18	69	1981	1	75
1956	11	74	1982	-13	70
1957	14	80	1983	-1	69
1958	16	77	1984	2	68
1959	30	81	1985	12	64
1960	28	83	1986	14	42
1961	21	80	1987	37	42
1962	18	79	1988	27	43
1963	30	78	1989	28	41
1964	27	78	1990	20	61
1965	12	87	1991	17	97
1966	13	78	1992	27	69
1967	32	88	1993	26	89
1968	36	82	1994	38	91
1969	30	79	1995	29	79
1970	25	70	1996	31	113
1971	12	73	1997	36	101
1972	20	62	1998	37	94

Table A.2 Classifications for Figures 6.4 and 6.5

Industry classification.

ANZIC	ASIC	CCLI	ASIC Industry title
Sector 1. Firms involved in the direct production of research and development, advertising, marketing and promotion of production, the industry or the firm, workplace and financial reform and improvement for profit.			
151	161	088, 086	Mineral exploration
7519	6172	609	Services to finance and investment nec
7520	6240	590	Services to insurance
7842	6372	742	Accounting services
7831, 7832	6381	746	Data processing services, information storage and retrieval
7851, 7852, 7853	6382	745	Advertising services
7854, 7855	6383	749	Market and business consultancy services
7810,	8461		Research and scientific institutions
962	847	744	Business and professional associations, Labour associations
7861	8491	609	Employment services
Sector 2. Other enterprises producing for profit.			
			All other codes not listed elsewhere
Sector 3. Non-profit sector (government and other) involved in the production of education, training, data collection and dissemination.			
841, 842	823	730	School education
843, 844	824	731, 732, 733, 734	Post school education
921, 922	825	739, 735, 739	Libraries, museums and art galleries
Sector 4. Other non-profit sector establishments.			
811	711	650, 651	Government administration
812	712		Justice
813	713	652	Foreign government representation
961	830	690, 691, 692	Welfare and religious institutions
7829	8462		Research and meteorological services

	848		Other community organisations
9631	8492	680	Police
9632	8493	681	Prisons and reformatories
9633	8494	683	Fire brigades
9634	8495		Sanitary and garbage disposal services
923	9141	758	Parks and zoological gardens

Sector 5. Defence.

820	720	660, 661, 662, 669, 670, 671, 672, 679	Defence

Occupational Classification

ASCO 2nd Ed (1997)	ASCO 1st Ed (1986)	ASCO 1st Ed title

Occupational group 1. Those that directly produce products which embody intangible assets in other people or other intangible forms. These include teachers, trainers, sales and marketing workers, management consultants, research and development staff, financial advisors and people involved in the collection, retrieval and dissemination of information and knowledge.

ASCO 2nd Ed (1997)	ASCO 1st Ed (1986)	ASCO 1st Ed title
24	24	School teachers
	25	Other teachers and instructors
11	12	General managers
12	13	Specialist managers
22, 32	27	Business professionals
253	28	Artists and related professionals
2522	2901	Economists
	2905	Educational researchers and related professionals
2523, 2529	2907	Other social scientists
	2909	Mathematicians, statisticians and actuaries
	2911	Librarians
	2999	Other professionals
591, 599, 614, 615, 619	52, 53, 54, 55, 59	Clerical workers
6211	6201	Sales representatives

Occupational group 2. Those who as a byproduct of their work experience acquire useful and relevant skills, knowledge and talents that contribute towards the goodwill, marketing and process efficiency of the enterprise or establishment.

13	14	Farmers and farm managers
33	15	Managing supervisors (sales and service)
	16	Managing supervisors (other business)
21	21	Natural scientists
	22	Building professional
23	23	Health diagnosis and treatment practitioners
2500, 251, 2520, 2521, 254	26	Social professionals
31	31	Medical and science technical officers and technicians
	32	Engineering and building associates and technicians
	33	Air and sea transport technical workers
34	34	Registered nurses
39	39	Miscellaneous para-professionals

Occupational group 3. Other occupations.

		All other codes not listed elsewhere

7 The Firm's Investment Decision

Introduction

Issues relating to price setting and production often overshadow microeconomic investment theory, in both post-Keynesian and neoclassical theory (see, for example, Lavoie 1992, Ch. 3). Investment remains behind the scenes as the model focuses on the short-run objectives of the firm and where treated it is depicted as the decision over whether to enhance and replenish productive capacity. Indicators of the need for more productive capacity include changes in demand for output, changes in total profits and changes in the market capitalisation of the firms relative to cost of replacement. Constraints on investment from the supply of funds and interest rates are rated highly by post-Keynesians but are excluded from neoclassical models by a perfect capital market assumption. According to Kalecki's principle of increasing risk, the more a firm seeks to borrow, the greater the default and bankruptcy risk and the higher compensating interest rates demanded by lenders. Banks' willingness-to-lend depends on their assessment of the firm's ability to service the loan from profits and their collateral in case of default.

Our discussion so far has suggested that the investment decision of firms is much broader than this. Firms undertake investment not only to extend productive capacity, but also to increase their control and knowledge over their internal and external environment. In this chapter we will suggest a microeconomic model which incorporates these additional motives, while also retaining the attractive and essential uncertainty assumptions found in post-Keynesian models.[1] We retain the notion of lenders' risk and, as such, the availability of investment funds depends on past profits and current collateral. We also use the rule of thumb adopted by Kalecki and many others, of basing the firm's expectations on its current circumstances. This has been persuasively justified by Keynes who argued that when uncertainty prevails, expectations are heavily biased towards what people know for certain, rather than speculations based on flimsy and incomplete information. This expectations formation rule is a common systematic force underlying firm behaviour.[2]

Our model uses a conventional optimising format. This does not imply that choices, on average, objectively reflect the most *ex post* profitable investment position for the firm. The parameters of the model are subjective and not necessarily unbiased estimates of the 'true' state of the world. The more insecure the firm feels about its own estimates the greater will be the risk premium required before it will agree to undertake an investment, *ceteris paribus*. In addition, we test how the firm should react, according to the model, under both variations in the trade cycle and in response to longer-term changes to the cost of production and intensity of competition.

A model of the microeconomic investment decision

In Chapter 5 we argued that a profit-maximising firm would seek to maximise its (monopoly) profits by investing in technical and market knowledge and demand-side and cost-side barriers to entry. Selection of a preferred price–quantity of output is a subordinate decision that is implied within each investment choice.[3] We may extend this basic principle to encompass investments to exploit market expansions, which arise from macroeconomic growth by increasing productive capacity.

For our problem, we will apply well-established non-linear programming techniques. The maximand is the present value of the *expected* additional profits (revenues less variable and fixed costs) Π^e, arising from a proposed investment activity. Two choice variables, I_{kc} and I_{ca} , investment in knowledge and control capital and capacity capital, exist. Knowledge capital refers to the accumulated knowledge and information-processing skills of the firm's workforce, control capital relates to the firm's firm-specific attributes which give it a cost or monopoly power advantage over its rivals and capacity capital determines the maximum level of output the firms can produce each period. We have grouped knowledge and control capital together as they are both motivated by the same motives: competition and uncertainty. The degree to which investment in either of these capitals is expected to raise the profitability of the firm depends on its appraisal of the economic situation. In keeping with Kalecki's principle of increasing risk there is one inequality constraint, a limit to the supply of investment funds which we denote as I^*.[4] Formally, our problem for each period is to

maximise $\qquad \Pi^e = R^e - C^e = h\left(I_{kc}, I_{ca}, \dfrac{dX}{dt}\right) - g\left(I_{kc}, I_{ca}\right)$ $\qquad$ (7.1)

subject to $\qquad\qquad\qquad I_{kc} + I_{ca} \le I^*.$

Using a dummy variable s, this can be transformed into an equality constraint,

$$I_{kc} + I_{ca} + s = I^*$$

and

$$I_{kc}, I_{ca}, s \geq I^*.$$

Where

Π^e = the present value of expected firm profits from proposed investment activities

R^e = the present value of expected firm revenues less running costs from the proposed investment activities

C^e = the present value of the expected capital costs of proposed investment activities

I_{kc} = proposed level of investment expenditure in knowledge and control capital

I_{ca} = proposed level of investment expenditure in capacity capital

X = events exogenous to the firms which affect profits, such as change to the macroeconomic level of activity, changes to consumer preferences, government regulations

P_t = actual gross profits flows in the period t

s = dummy or slack variable

h, g are the functional forms for R^e and C^e respectively.

The present value of expected revenues from a given asset or a given investment vintage can be summed using an infinite geometric series.[5] We may represent gross profits in each period as a function of the level of capital services flowing from each firms stock of capital. These profits are net of wage and raw material costs which we take as given. This can be represented as

$$P^e_{t+1} = f_1\left(K^s_t\right) \text{ and } \frac{dP^e_{t+1}}{dt} = f_1\left(\frac{dK^s_t}{dt}\right) \tag{7.2}$$

where P^e_{t+1} represents profits the firm expects to receive in the next period if the proposed investment activity proceeds and K^s represents all capital services. The level of capital services in each period depends on both the past investments in each type of capital asset as well as the uncontrollable exogenous factors included under X. Thus the change in capital services in each period depends on the last period's investment and exogenous events:

$$\frac{dK^s}{dt} = f_2\left(I_{kc}, I_{ca}, \frac{dX}{dt}\right)$$

and

$$\frac{dP^e_{t+1}}{dt} = f_1\left[f_2\left(I_{kc}, I_{ca}, \frac{dX}{dt}\right)\right] = f\left(I_{kc}, I_{co}, \frac{dX}{dt}\right).$$

Dividing by π, the discount factor, reduces the one period addition to (gross) profits to a capitalised present value:

$$R^e = \frac{\left[dP^e_{t+1}/dt\right]}{\pi} = \frac{f_1\left[dK^s/dt\right]}{\pi} = \frac{f\left[I_{kc}, I_{ca}, (dX/dt)\right]}{\pi} \qquad (7.3)$$

Where π is the gross discount rate such that, $\pi = x + i + \delta$, and x is the discount factor for risk-aversion which equals the firms (tolerance of uninsured-single-instance risk) × (the level of uninsured-single-instance risk) + (tolerance of uncertainty) × (perception of uncertainty). i is the default free interest rate (overnight or cash rate) and δ is the rate of depreciation. Any increase in the level of perceived uncertainty will reduce the estimated benefits from a proposed investment.

The function f represents the sensitivity of extra *expected* profits for a given change in investment of a particular type. This function must represent the firm's best guess as to the effectiveness of expanding each type of asset. There is no presumption that *ex post* the choice is unbiased and optimal. Because it takes time to acquire knowledge and process information, and because it takes time to change consumer spending patterns, the culture of the workplace and the process of production, the firm expects that there will be diminishing additional profits to investment within any given time period. The higher is our level of investment within any given period, the further we push into unfamiliar and uncertain territory, and the lower are the expected marginal returns.

To derive C^e, the expected capital cost of the proposed investment, we will assume that expected capital costs are equal to actual capital costs and that all capital costs will be incurred in a single period. In addition, we define each unit of investment good to be normalised at a cost of £1 and this price, by our earlier assumption, does not vary over the trade cycle. I_i represents both the cost of each additional unit of capital and the number of additional units of capital. Consequently

$$C^e{}_t = I_{kc_t} + I_{ca_t}$$

and from equation (7.1)

$$\Pi^e{}_t = \frac{f\left[I_{kc_t}, I_{ca_t}, (dX/dt)\right]}{\pi} - \left(I_{kc_{t+1}} + I_{ca_t}\right).$$

The Lagrangian function for the model is

$$Z = \frac{f\left[I_{kc_t}, I_{ca_t}, (dX/dt)\right]}{\pi} - \left(I_{kc_t} + I_{ca_t}\right) + \lambda\left[I^* - \left(I_{kc_t} + I_{ca_t}\right) - s\right].$$

The first-order conditions (or Kuhn-Tucker conditions) for an optimal microeconomic investment decision within each time period, require that (and dropping the time subscripts for convenience)[6]

$$\frac{\partial Z}{\partial_{kc}} = \frac{f_{I_{kc}}}{\pi} - 1 - \lambda \leq 0, \quad I_k \geq 0$$

and

$$I_k\left(\frac{f_{I_k}}{\pi} - 1 - \lambda\right) = 0$$

$$\frac{\partial Z}{\partial_{ca}} = \frac{f_{I_{ca}}}{\pi} - 1 - \lambda \leq 0, \quad I_{ca} \geq 0,$$

and

$$I_{ca}\left(\frac{f_{I_{ca}}}{\pi} - 1 - \lambda\right) = 0$$

and

$$\frac{\partial Z}{\partial \lambda} = I^* - (I_{kc} + I_{ca}) \geq 0, \quad \lambda \geq 0, \text{ and } \lambda\left[I^* - (I_{kc} + I_{ca})\right] = 0 \quad (7.4).$$

Where $f_{I_{kc}}$, $f_{I_{ca}}$ are partial derivatives of f with respect to I_{kc}, I_{ca}.

In this case λ is the shadow price of the marginal unit of investment finance which rises with investment levels, $\partial Z / \partial I_i$ is the marginal present value of profits of an extra capital of type i, 1 (by assumption) is the amount of investment units required to create an extra unit of asset i, and $\lambda \times 1$ represents the cost of investment (including the scarcity of investment funds) used to create an extra unit of asset i. If the financial constraint is not met, then by equation (7.4), $\lambda = 0$.

To intuitively understand the implications of these conditions we will consider the specific example of investment activity in knowledge capital. The Kuhn-Tucker conditions require either that $I_{kc} = 0$ and/or that $f_{I_{kc}} / \pi - 1 - \lambda = 0$. If we take $I_{kc} = 0$ (or $I_{ca} = 0$) to be an economically extreme case, then the second condition usually applies. The optimal level of investment in knowledge capital will be met when $f_{I_{kc}} / \pi = 1 + \lambda$.

The left-hand side represents the present value of marginal revenue and the right-hand side represents the present value of marginal cost of investing in knowledge capital. These conditions hold only for one time period and parameters for subsequent decisions are determined afresh in subsequent periods. The only linkages between periods are the effects of realised results of past investments on current expectation, and the effects of past profits on the financial constraint (λ). Figure 7.1 represents this graphically. When the financial constraint is met , $\lambda > 0$, and the levels of investment in each form of capital are reduced. The level of investment in capacity capital are derived in a similar manner.

*Figure 7.1 Present value of marginal cost and marginal revenue from
investing in knowledge and control assets*

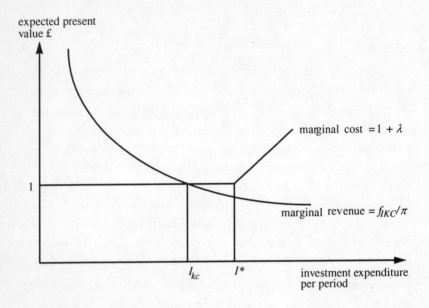

Cycle effects

To use our set of profit-maximising equations we will assume a specific functional form for the expected profits equation (7.2). We assume that the services from the capital assets must be applied in fixed proportions. This assumption need not hold strictly, but our explanation is clearer if we abstract from variable proportions.

The various forms of investment discussed in Chapter 3 have been categorised in a way to emphasise their complementarity in the production and sale of commodities, that is the process of acquiring profits. Knowledge capital is generally considered antecedent to the successful accumulation of capacity and control goods. Without technical knowledge and understanding, the firm has limited ability to establish a viable productive unit, without knowledge about the way specific markets and industries operate, it will experience difficulty establishing a foothold in output markets. Similarly, without these established footholds and ability to market output, the firm has no need for productive capacity. Without a basic level of productive efficiency, the firm will have no market for its output and also no need for productive capacity.

Some capital goods will have two or more properties, which place them within the confines of more than one type of asset. Innovations can both expand capacity and give the firm a unique cost advantage. Investments into market control also enhance one's knowledge of an industry. However, we will appeal to the reader to abstract from these complexities in order to make the argument in this section more transparent.

Accordingly, let us assume that the desired ratio of asset services implies a desired ratio of capital $zK_{kc} : K_{ca}$ being the present value of knowledge, control and capacity capital respectively. To accept this assumption we need to believe that a certain ratio of services from knowledge and control capital are required in order to get the best expected profit per unit of raw product. These services provide the knowledge and skills and systems of support which transform an object (including an intangible object) into a valued commodity. If the state of knowledge changes then not enough knowledge capital services will be forthcoming from the given knowledge capital as they currently stand. If other firms alter their behaviour and invest in additional marketing, distribution, design, rent-seeking or cost-minimising strategies, then not enough control capital services will flow through to support the product. The expected profit per output will be suboptimal.

Let us define a unit of a complete dose of capital services as K^s_d where a complete dose of capital services is defined as

$$K^s_d = \min\left(\frac{1}{z}K^s_{kc}, K^s_{ca}\right).$$

Hence

$$\frac{dK^s_d}{dt} = \frac{dK^s_{ca}}{dt} \quad \text{if } K^s_{ca} < \frac{1}{z}K^s_{kc}$$

$$= \frac{dK^s_{kc}}{dt} \quad \text{if } K^s_{ca} > \frac{1}{z}K^s_{kc}$$

$$= \frac{d\left(K^s_{ca} + zK^s_{kc}\right)}{dt} \quad \text{if } K^s_{ca} = K^s_{kc}$$

and

$$\frac{dK^s_{ca}}{dt} = f_3(I_{ca}) \text{ if } K^s_{ca} < \frac{1}{z}K^s_{kc}$$

$$\frac{dK^s_{kc}}{dt} = f_4\left[I_{kc},(dX/dt)\right] \text{ if } K^s_{ca} > \frac{1}{z}K^s_{kc}$$

$$\frac{d\left(K^s_{ca} + zK^s_{kc}\right)}{dt} = f_5\left[I_{ca}, zI_{kc}, z(dX/dt)\right] \text{ if } K^s_{ca} = \frac{1}{z}K^s_{kc}.$$

If we assume that $f = \left[(dK^s_d / dt)\right]^\varepsilon$, then from (7.3), the present value of the net revenue function may be expressed as

$$R^e = \frac{(I_{ca})^\varepsilon}{\pi} \quad \text{if } K^s_{ca} < \frac{1}{z}K^s_{kc}$$

$$= \frac{\left[I_{kc} + (dX/dt)\right]^\varepsilon}{\pi} \quad \text{if } K^s_{ca} > \frac{1}{z}K^s_{kc}$$

$$= \frac{\left[I_{ca} + zI_{kc} + x(dX/dt)\right]^\varepsilon}{\pi} \quad \text{if } K^s_{ca} = K^s_{kc}$$

where $\varepsilon < 1$, for diminishing profitability to additional doses of investment per time period are still assumed to operate because of the time it takes firms to acquire knowledge and control the behaviour of consumers, rivals, suppliers of inputs and the government.

Each complete dose of investment costs £ $(1 + z)$.

Our new Lagrangians are

$$Z = \frac{(I_{ca})^\varepsilon}{\pi} - I_{ca}(1+z) + \lambda(I^* - I_{ca}(1+z) - s) \text{ if } K^s_{ca} < \frac{1}{z}K^s_{kc}$$

$$= \frac{\left[I_{kc} + (dX/dt)\right]^\varepsilon}{\pi} - I_{ca}(1+z) + \lambda(I^* - I_{ca}(1+z) - s) \text{ if } K^s_{ca} > \frac{1}{z}K^s_{kc}$$

$$= \frac{\left[I_{ca} + zI_{kc} + z(dX/dt)\right]^\varepsilon}{\pi} - I_{ca}(1+z) + \lambda(I^* - I_{ca}(1+z) - s) \text{ if } K^s_{ca} = K^s_{kc}.$$

These give several optimal levels of investment expenditure I, depending on the initial assessment of the ratio of forthcoming capital services.

Accordingly:

$$I = I_{ca} = \left[\frac{\varepsilon}{(1+\lambda)\pi}\right]^{\{1/1-\varepsilon\}} \quad \text{if } K^s{}_{ca} < \frac{1}{z}K^s{}_{kc} \tag{7.5}$$

$$I = I_{kc} = \left[\frac{z}{z^{\{1/1-\varepsilon\}}}\right]\left[\frac{\varepsilon}{(1+\lambda)\pi}\right]^{\{1/1-\varepsilon\}} \quad \text{if } K^s{}_{ca} > \frac{1}{z}K^s{}_{kc} \tag{7.6}$$

$$I_{ca} = \left[\frac{1}{(1+z)^{\{1/1-\varepsilon\}}}\right]\left[\frac{\varepsilon}{(1+\lambda)\pi}\right]^{\{1/1-\varepsilon\}} \quad \text{if } K^s{}_{ca} = \frac{1}{z}K^s{}_{kc} \tag{7.7a}$$

and

$$I_{kc} = \left[\frac{z}{(1+z)^{\{1/1-\varepsilon\}}}\right]\left[\frac{\varepsilon}{(1+\lambda)\pi}\right]^{\{1/1-\varepsilon\}} \tag{7.7b}$$

such that

$$I = I_{ca} + I_{kc} = \left[\frac{1+z}{(1+z)^{\{1/1-\varepsilon\}}}\right]\left[\frac{\varepsilon}{(1+\lambda)\pi}\right]^{\{1/1-\varepsilon\}} \tag{7.7}.$$

ε is an expectational coefficient, which reflects the expected profitability of maintaining the level of capital assets and the confidence and competitive drive, imbued in members of the firm. It indicates their assumed ability to steal market share or cause their own market to grow relative to the whole economy. λ represents the constraint on the firm's access to funds which according to the discussion above on lender's risk, reflects last period's flow of profits. I is the total level of investment expenditure on both type of capital asset.

Macroeconomic growth

Several situations exist when one or two of the separate capital assets will be subject to capital loss or gain, which are relevant to our macrodynamic model. Once-off changes to the macroeconomy will lead to a change in X and firms will experience a gain or loss of control and knowledge capital through events exogenous to their own efforts. At higher levels of demand, the value of the firm's market and technical knowledge rises because the potential profit flows from control and knowledge capital rises. Were the firm able to find the means for extra capacity, then the value of the knowledge and control capital would rise. Similarly, a rise in market demand will increase the value of the firm's ability to sell, distribute and reach high income (or willing-to-pay) consumers, and the value of its ability to organise production efficiently and use best practice technologies and practices. Accordingly, when demand does rise, the firm believes that it can expand the production of the raw product without any loss of profit per unit of output. In effect, control capital has increased in value.[7]

There will be two effects on our micro-decision equations. First, firms which previously had the desired balance of capital services will tend to become firms with a shortage of capacity capital. Secondly, a higher level of profits will lower the shadow price of investment finance and thus raise the desired level of capital over all.

The first effect lead to a rise in both total investment and capacity investment as the implied level of investment under macroeconomic expansion (equation (7.5)) is higher that the level when existing capital services are in balance (equation (7.7)). This follows because $\varepsilon < 1$ and thus

$$\frac{1+z}{(1+z)^{\{1/1-\varepsilon\}}} < 1.$$

The second factor affecting the level of total investment expenditure in macroeconomic upswing comes through the firm's enhanced assess to investment finance. A stronger flow of profits leads to a fall in λ and a higher level of investment expenditure.

Macroeconomic contraction

The effects of a macroeconomic contraction on the value of services from knowledge and control capital is the reverse situation. A once-off change in the perceived level of uncertainty will, using the same logic as above, lead to a gain or loss of knowledge capital services. Assume that X rises as a fall in the magnitude of aggregate profits manifests itself as an across the board fall in each firm's demand function. For similar reasons to the expansion case, two separate effects will operate. First, there will be a loss to knowledge and control capital and secondly, there will be a rise in the shadow price of investment finance. In the first case, the firm's flow of knowledge and control services falls below the optimal level given its supply of capacity services. The short-period equilibrium condition assumes that firms immediately respond to a fall in demand by cutting back on production, and a surplus of productive capacity capital emerges.

Under this situation the implied level of investment in knowledge and control capital is implied in equation (7.6). This can explain why investment is still positive even during severe contractions and why Marx observed that during the downturn of a trade cycle, firms compete harder as they scavenge for falling aggregate profits.

If we also include the effect of a rise in the shadow price of investment finance λ then, depending on the sensitivity of λ to profits, the aggregate level of investment will fall, as we may intuitively expect.

When there is a once-off change in competitive pressure from, for example, government policy, a surplus of productive capacity emerges and knowledge and control investment are encouraged, but there is no fall in the firm's access to investment finance. Because the change in competitive pressure has not been caused by the fall in aggregate profits, the shadow price of investment finance λ does not alter.

Uncertainty

Similar reasoning can be applied in the case of a rise in the level of uncertainty due either to a sudden turn in the economy or to factors exogenous to the private sector economy. A rise in uncertainty may cause both a fall in services from firms' knowledge capital and a rise in the risk/uncertainty discount factor x, in π. The first effect causes an excess of capacity capital. Total investment in this case is purely in knowledge and control capital, however, the magnitude of total investment expenditures is tempered by a rise in the risk and uncertainty discount factor x. The net effect on investment is theoretically ambiguous.

We have deleted the time subscripts merely to avoid clutter, but it must be remembered that each investment decision relates to only one time period. Whether investment rises, falls or remains the same depends on the levels in the next period. We will argue in the next chapter that this depends on the *ex post* macroeconomic effects of decisions made in the current period.

Long term changes

Falling costs of tangible capital

As the relevance of intangible capital assets is increasingly discussed in the literature it is tempting to think that physical capital is becoming less important for the production of goods and services. However, 'importance' depends on one's perspective especially given the distinction between the use-value of a factor and its exchange-value. If tangible and intangible capital are complements in production, then a debate over which is more important or has become more important, is relatively fruitless. Implements without skills and labour produce nothing and there are few commodities which can only be produced with skilled labour alone. A debate over the intrinsic value of each type of capital is like discussing whether food or water is more necessary for human survival.

Nevertheless, we have reasonable evidence from Chapter 6 that the relative sum of *exchange-values* of intangible capital has risen over the last half century. Price relates to the difficulty of reproduction at the margin rather than the usefulness of the total factor. As discussed in Chapter 5, one of the features of intangible capital is that it is inherently heterogeneous. As a competitive device to create market barriers to entry, it is meant to be heterogeneous. Much intangible capital is embodied in the workforce and people are inherently heterogeneous. An efficient manager or work team cannot be as easily reproduced over and over again no matter how long the time profile and investments, which are embodied in labour, can accordingly be subject to rising marginal costs. By contrast, tangible capital can be reproduced at a standard quality *ad nauseum*. If we invent a successful machine, we can keep producing more and more of exactly the same type of machine at a constant cost, given time. The very uniformity of machines makes it subject to efficiency improvements through the division of labour and more mechanised or roundabout techniques of production.

There are no existing indices of the relative cost of tangible to intangible capital. Part of the difficulty of construction such as index lies in the practical problems associated with defining and measuring a standard service, but there is also a problem in valuing many intermediate services which are produced for the firms' own account. A comparison of price indices for tangible plant and equipment with the Consumer Price Index (which incorporates consumption services) is the closest ratio we can find for the relative price of intangible investment services to tangible investment items. Figure 7.2 shows that this there has been a marked downward trend in this ratio in Australia since 1961.

Our model also shows how a falling cost of tangible capital relative to intangible capital can cause firms to commit more investment expenditure toward intangible commodities.

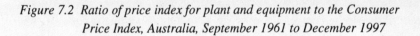

Figure 7.2 Ratio of price index for plant and equipment to the Consumer Price Index, Australia, September 1961 to December 1997

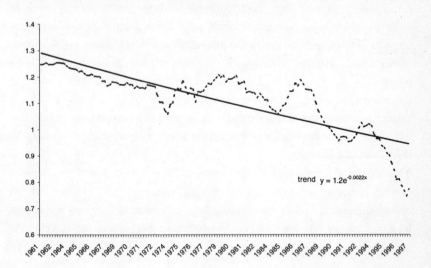

According to equation (7.7), the ratio of investment expenditure in productive capacity to control and knowledge capital over the long term is:

$$\frac{I_{ca}}{I_{kc}} = \frac{1}{z}$$

Given that most tangible capital is undertaken to enhance productive capacity, if the cost per unit per I_{ca} falls (or the number of units per £1 rises) then z rises and the level of relative expenditure on capacity capital falls relative to control and knowledge investment, which are mainly embodied in the firm's workforce.[8] A fall in the relative level of a firm's tangible assets is expected to reduce the firm's relative level of collateral and increase the shadow price of finance λ. This will depress the overall level of investment expenditure for firms of a given profit stream.

Higher sustained levels of competition
The situation of an unanticipated once-off rise in competitive pressure is akin to a once-off fall X. The depreciation rate, which rises if there is an anticipated and continual decline in the flow of capital services is not affected. However, if firms experience a sustained rise in competitive pressure they will have to continually invest in additional knowledge and

control capital each period in order to keep demand continually at its former level. If the rise in competitive pressure is brought about by the entry of new firms (say due to a lowering of tariffs or other government regulations), incumbent firms find they have to invest in more control capital, such as marketing, cost reduction and so on in order either to squeeze out these new entrants or to extend the size of the market. Firms face a sink or swim choice. Either they leave the industry or they lower their aversion to risk and uncertainty and remain in the industry. In the latter case they lower the required premium to compensate them for the risks of doing business. This is similar to the short-period price analysis. When price competition rises, firms can either lower their price and accept a lower rate of profit or simply be priced out of business.

The effect of a reduction of the premium for risk is to lower the required rate of profit π, which raises the present value of net revenues for an investment and the profit-maximising level of complete doses of investment increases (from equation (7.7)). If firms take the option of quitting the industry, competitive pressure eases.

Conclusion

If we accept the postulates that

1. firms seek to maximise the present values of their capital, that is the present value of the future stream of expected profits, both normal and monopoly,
2. normal profits are earned by keeping up with industry standards of efficiency and market power and monopoly profits are obtained by successfully erecting endogenous barriers to entry and by decreasing the firm's perception of uncertainty and uninsured-single-instance risks,[9] and
3. successful and hard-to-emulate endogenous barriers and reductions to the degree of felt uncertainty are made by intangible investments, especially control capital in league with knowledge capital,

then we may represent the investment decision as an integral part of the firm's constrained profit-maximising behaviour for each separate time period. If we classify our investment goods so their contribution to the process of accruing profits are perfect complements, then we can derive separate and additive investment–decision equations. Each separate investment decision depends on the current size of the firm's profits which determines the ready availability of finance for its investment activities (λ), expectations of increasing the profitability of the firm by investment activity (ε), and the extent of underutilisation of the other type of capital. Furthermore, depicting our profit function in this form allows us to explain why some firms continue to invest during cyclical downturns.

While these equations may have some value for an analysis of the microeconomic investment decision, they are not presented in a form which allows us to incorporate the effects of last period's *ex post* macroeconomic outcomes. We would ideally want to transform the relations so that they mimic the economic analysis of the proceeding chapters without using extraneous mathematical approximations. This is not easy, and the next chapter makes a rudimentary attempt to do so.

Notes

[1] As discussed in Chapter 4, the assumptions of fundamental uncertainty and the process of competition effectively exclude game theory analysis.

[2] For example, when the firm makes a capital gain on its last period's investment, it takes this as an indication that there are further exploitable investments opportunities available. Because of uncertainty, firms only know a single point on an Marginal Efficiency of Capital function and they must estimate the shape of the Marginal Efficiency of Capital from this point.

[3] An estimate of a price and output level has to be made in order to estimate the present value of each investment option.

[4] Accordingly, as a matter of mathematical convenience, this interprets Kalecki's financial constraint as an absolute limit instead of a spongy barrier, which may be penetrated upon payment of a penalty rate of interest.

[5] We chose in Chapter 4 to allow the firm's perception of uninsured risk and uncertainty to be reflected in the risk discount factor x, instead affecting the life of the asset. This choice is a matter of mathematical convenience but it does not alter the substance of what we are saying. When the degree of felt uncertainty is high, the contribution of marginally distant profit flows to the present value calculation is very small.

[6] So long as $f(I_{kc}, I_{ca})/\pi$ is concave function, the Kuhn-Tucker sufficiency conditions are automatically satisfied also.

[7] Thus there is no strict concept of full capacity utilisation for knowledge and control capital.

[8] This follows directly from the assumption of fixed factor proportions.

[9] The firm aims to avoid its own felt uncertainty but not that felt by its rivals.

8 Integration into Macrodynamics

Introduction

Aggregate profits and its twin aggregate investment propel macrodynamic theory through a mutually dependent interplay of means and ends. Profits are the means and motive for investment and investment is the source of profits. Given this, it is worth exploring the effects of altering the investment motive and outcomes by incorporating the additional feature of intangible capital. We have chosen to adapt Kalecki's macrodynamic model for our purpose because of its general clarity and clear logic.

We begin this chapter by transforming the microeconomic investment decision into a linear second-order difference equation. Ultimately we hope to make transparent the *ceteris paribus* dynamic motions of an economy where firms are motivated by the competition and uncertainty motives as well as the familiar capacity motive. Nonetheless, our adaptation of Kalecki's basic model does not change its fundamental properties, such as the existence of endogenous cycles and the dependence of the centre of gravitation on autonomous expenditures.

Kalecki's macrodynamics

The attraction of Kalecki's theories resides in their dynamic format that mimics the time sequence of a typical investment decision–action–effect–response path. *Ex post* profits and *ex ante* investment expenditure combine in an historical time process. Causation and outcome cannot be divorced from the temporal ordering of events and simultaneous solutions will not be indicative of the path of development. In Kalecki's macrodynamics, a reasonable expectation of future profits and a pool of accumulated funds are antecedent to the firm's investment decision, for funds which arrive as a result of the decision, or contemporaneously with a decision, can only affect next period's decision. It is our intention in this chapter to deliberate over how the *ex ante* microeconomic decision from the last chapter may be integrated with his after-the-event macroeconomic relationships.

According to our discussion so far, investments to extend the firm's productive capacity, investments designed to match or outperform rivals' level of proficiency and market position, or measures designed to moderate the firm's perception of uncertainty, depend on an expectation of returning a satisfactory profit. However, in Kalecki's schema, actual profits are mainly derived from the aggregate of firms' investment expenditures and a continual rise or fall of these forms of investments cannot be feasibly sustained on their own. Given this, a closed economy model can only grow if there is a growth in autonomous expenditures. In our model this incorporates the stable portion of capitalists' consumption expenditure and *ex niliho* investment expenditures. The latter probably reflects on a systematic basis, cultural factors which give particular societies confidence and creative energy. It is difficult to see how this factor would continually increase over time.[1]

While the private sector may confront an apparently unlimited potential for developing new ideas and new investment opportunities (even without major stimulus from the scientific sector), according to Kalecki's macroeconomic relationships, the profit incentive to develop these ideas is not unlimited and his theory does not support ideas of endogenous growth through technological change. While technical change may be a necessary condition for growth, sustainable growth also requires a growth in autonomous or the non-profit dependent end-use expenditures.

Kalecki's model may be expounded using three steps.

1. Kalecki employed assumptions to remove complicating details, which are neither endogenous to the task at hand nor large. Specifically, he assumed that
    - the economy is in continuous short period equilibrium,
    - there is no government sector,
    - the economy is closed,
    - workers do not save,
    - there is no time lag between income and consumption expenditure but there are lags between the recognition of an investment opportunity and actual investment expenditure,
    - there is a constant percentage mark-up on unit costs,
    - the money supply is endogenous, and
    - there are unemployed resources.

    The final assumption merely states that Kalecki's theories are demand-side theories, and were they to be applied to modern-day economic situations, with supply-side complications such as labour market partitioning (that is, unemployment hysteresis) or cost inflation, they may need to be modified.

2. Kalecki devised three key behavioural rules. First, that capitalists' consumption expenditure is a function of their profit income. Second, that investment demand is a function of expected profitability, which in turn is a function of current profitability. And finally, that under normal, prudential lending rules, lending institutions use the firm's existing stream of profits as a rule of thumb to partially determine how much they will lend for investment.
3. Given the first set of assumptions and the second set of rules, Kalecki derives a set of macro identities, which must hold at within each short period.

Output may be described as consisting of three sectors, the workers' consumption goods sector, the capitalists' consumption goods sector and the investment goods sector. The first set of assumptions gives us the basic identities (for any given short period t):

$$P \equiv C_K + S$$

$$W \equiv C_W$$

$$Y \equiv W + P \equiv C_W + C_K + S,$$

and the short-period equilibrium condition

$$S = I,$$

so that

$$Y = C_W + C_K + I.$$

Where

P = real aggregate profits, gross of amortisation and net of interest payments to/from the central bank
C_K = real aggregate capitalists' consumption expenditure
S = real aggregate saving, gross of amortisation (capital consumption)
W = real aggregate wages = $\omega(L/Y)Y$, where ω is the real hourly wage and L is hours of labour.
I = real aggregate investment, gross of depreciation
C_w = real aggregate workers' consumption expenditure, and

Y = real output.

His behavioural relationship for capitalists' consumption gives

$$C_K = \lambda P + A,$$

which in association with his identities and the short-period equilibrium condition, gives (inserting time subscripts)

$$P_t = m \, [\, I_t + A(t) \,], \tag{8.1}$$

Where A is the stable portion of capitalists' real consumption expenditure, which changes slowly over-time but not over the cycle, λ is capitalists' marginal propensity to consume. λ is a small fraction, such that $0 < \lambda < 1$, and m is $1/(1-\lambda) > 1$.

Because investment expenditures are the outcome of deliberate decisions and profits are not, he reasoned that I and A are the independent variables which determine P, and not vice versa. The unit period is the time taken for the entrepreneur to reconsider his/her investment decision on the basis of unexpected profits.

With substitutions we obtain

$$Y_t = W_t + \lambda \, P_t + A(t) + I.$$

Given $P_t \equiv Y_t - W_t$, then the short period equilibrium level of output is

$$Y_t = W + \frac{A(t) + I}{(1 - \lambda)}.$$

If the real wage, the output-labour ratio and the parameters of capitalists' consumption functions are exogenous, then aggregate investment demand equation I is the main determinant of the level of economic activity. It remains therefore to define this function.

The macro-micro interface

Assigning microeconomic foundations to macroeconomic models has, to date, largely involved using a representative firm model to underpin the macroeconomic model. A popular approach is to effectively scale up an individual agent model of individual choice by replacing individual prices and quantities with aggregate prices and quantities (see for example, Blanchard and Fischer 1989). It is also common to use aggregate equations which are not directly mathematically linked to the chosen microeconomic model. The latter exists only to foster an impression of theoretical soundness upon the discussion.

In contrast to these two positions, Kalecki's method, according to Kriesler, is a stepwise integration of both macro and micro relationships (Kriesler 1989). Results from each level of analysis feed in as determinants of the other. Aggregate investment in each period is the sum of the micro decisions based on each firm's assessment of the current situation and its own motivations. These decisions combine to determine the macroeconomic outcome in each period. However, these microeconomic assessments and motivations are influenced by outcomes from the last period which in aggregate are determined purely by macroeconomic considerations. Effectively, the micro equation models the motives inducing economic activity while the macro equations provide the constraints due to the interaction and outcome of these forces.

In Kalecki's macro scheme, realised changes to profits result only from changes in aggregate expenditure, such that from equation (8.1), $dP_t = m(dA_t + dI_t) + (A_t + I_t)dm$. However, at the micro level, each firm bases its own investment decision on what it believes *it* can do individually to promote its own profits. With this in mind, the level and type of investment expenditure will be based on how effective the firm believes it will be in achieving markets sales *vis-à-vis* competitors and market requirements. Unintentionally, however, the firm's decision will have macroeconomic implications that affect the realisation of its expectations and thus its future decisions.

Kalecki's 1968 microeconomic investment decision equation was based solely upon the productive capacity motive. According to this limited view, firms invest either in response to a rise in profitability, or, to offset physical deterioration in existing structures and equipment. Kalecki represented this by his equation

$$I_{t+\tau} = jI_t + r\left(\frac{n\Delta P_t + \delta P_t}{\pi} - I_t\right) + B(t). \qquad (8.2)$$

Where

$I_{t+\tau}$ = the level of investment expenditure decided upon in period t and executed in period $t+\tau$

π = the gross required rate of profit (as defined above), $\pi > 0$

r = measure of entrepreneurs confidence, $r > 0$

j = portion of profits retained by firms, $0 < j < 1$

δ = rate of obsolescence due to technical progress, $\delta > 0$

n = the pro rata share of additional profits captured the new investment in the absence of technological progress, $0 < n < 1$

$B(t)$ = the effect innovation has on entrepreneurs who expect to capture rents from being the first in the field to innovate.

This equation has three additive components. The first deals with the availability of investment finance for the firm. The risk of default limits the readiness of financial intermediaries to lend to the firm for further investment.

The second component 'is based on the idea that entrepreneurs scrutinise how the new investment is "doing" in terms of profitability. . . [and further investment] depends on whether the expected rate of return on new investment proves to be equal to, higher, or lower that the "standard rate" π' (Kalecki 1968, 442). In this component, r represents entrepreneurs' reaction coefficient, $(n\Delta P_t + \delta P_t)/\pi$ indicates the present value of estimated net revenues from the asset (current revenues less current costs),[2] and I_t is the capital cost of the asset. Expressed as such, it is parallel to Tobin's q except there is no implication that the present value reflects the stock exchange valuation and Tobin uses a ratio and Kalecki a difference. If the present value of net revenues is greater than the capital or investment cost, then a capital gain is, on balance, expected and investment spending is encouraged, *ceteris paribus*. If it is less, investment is discouraged. This equation embodies a vintage notion of capital assets for δP reflects the retirement rate of the oldest vintages.

The last component $B(t)$, represents the additional stimulus to investment due to the belief by the entrepreneur that his or her firm will be the first in the field with an innovation.

Incorporating intangible investment into this model will have two effects. First, only a limited portion of intangible investment actively leads to mortgagable collateral. Accordingly, the firm's ability to borrow falls over time if it invests in a rising potion of intangible capital. Second, there are two motives for investment in additional to the standard productive capacity motive and this must be taken account of. Kalecki took uncertainty and imperfect knowledge to be pervasive and parts of his investment decision equations already include behaviours to moderate the ill effects of uncertainty and risk.

Firm's cost of investment funds

Whether the firm has the option of investing at all depends on its ability to raise funds prior to investment and the firm's perception of its own ability to successfully undertake these investments. Without credible evidence of successful business behaviour or marketable collateral, firms generally experience difficulty finding lenders at a normal market rate of interest.

Normal prudential lending practices require, first, that firms show evidence of being able to service a loan and, secondly, that firms can provide security in the case of bankruptcy. Serviceability is usually assessed by the firm's recent profit record. Security is assessed by the firm's property, the legal title of which is assigned to the mortgagee. Retained profits and net tangible assets (NTA) commonly form this property and in some cases limited intangible capital assets such as patents may be included.

The contemporary practice of taxing interest incomes but allowing tax deductions for interest payments, reinforces the desire by controlling shareholders to expand and invest using debt rather than equity finance. If firms feel that acquirable assets, which will sustain their value, exist, borrowing to buy an asset is more profitable than accumulating wealth by saving. This does not amount to an automatic re-investment of savings. When doubts exist about the future value of reproducible capital, re-investment will fall short of savings.[3]

While Kalecki discussed the importance of both the flow of profits and the net asset position of the firm in an earlier work (Kalecki [1939], 1990, 292, 306–8). he reduced this feature in his 1968 paper to a single variable, which reflects the flow of profits only. Both this reduction in scope and the convention that only tangible assets comprise acceptable collateral, suggest a need to re-examine the presentation of his 'principle of increasing risk'.[4] In the *Essays in the Theory of Economic Fluctuations*, Kalecki ([1939], 1990) argued that investment finance could be provided through

- retained earnings due to past profits,
- loans from financial intermediaries and rentiers, and
- new equity issues.

The first two factors, profit flows and retained earnings, may be represented as a portion of current profits. We will assume that the second factor also depends on the firm's NTA (plus measured intangible assets) or collateral.[5] Following our empirical findings in Chapter 6, we will assume that this declines as a proportion of the total value of the firm over time.

Not only debt but also sources of equity finance are subject to natural limits according to the level of uncertainty in the market. Kalecki argued that both rentiers risk aversion and internal resistance by the incumbent controlling shareholders will limit the extent of new equity issues.[6] We expect that firms with high levels of intangible assets will tend to rely more on internal sources of finance.[7] However, financial intermediaries may respond to a secular fall in firms' NTAs by relaxing the weight given to this factor when assessing a firm's loan worthiness. Nevertheless, for the remainder of this chapter, we assume that banks use the firm's NTA and disregard any secular rise in the portion of intangible assets.

Given that the value of a firm's existing assets is P^e/π, then

$$\text{NTA} = a_1 e^{a_2 t}\left(\frac{P^e}{\pi}\right).$$

If we accept the myopic rule for decision making under uncertain conditions, $P^e = P$, then together with the influence from the firm's current profit flows, the firm's supply of investment finance in the current period t, can be expressed as a function of last period's profits, such that

$$I^*_t = a_0 P_{t-1} + a_3 a_1 e^{a_2 t}\left(\frac{P_{t-1}}{\pi}\right). \tag{8.3}$$

Where

a_0 = reflects the sensitivity of a firm's access to investment funds current profit flows.

a_1 = the proportion of tangible capital in total capital when $t = 0$.

a_2 = the per period rate of change in the proportion of a firm's NTA and measured intangibles.

a_3 = reflects the sensitivity of a firm's access to investment funds to its NTA.

In terms of our microeconomic model of the investment decision presented in Chapter 7, a change to the firm's level of profits, P will increase I^* and reduce the pressure on λ..

The macro investment equation

As mentioned above, there are well-recognised problems associated with aggregating over individual units. Formally, we can only sum or average the individual independent variables to get aggregate dependent variables if the micro equations are identical and linear (Green 1977, 190). If our microeconomic equations are non-linear, as ours are in Chapter 7, both the distribution of the independent variables across firms,[8] and the covariance between these variables affects the way the micro equation are summed to get an aggregate equation. To remove ourselves from these complications we need to accept a level of approximation.

We have chosen to model our macrodynamic *ex ante* investment equation by first separating out the influence of available investment finance from the expected profitability component, and secondly, by separately modelling the three motives for investment.

Availability of finance

The first element in our macroeconomic equation is a direct adaptation of equation

$$I^*_t = a_0 P_{t-1} + a_3 a_1 e^{a_2 t}\left(\frac{P_{t-1}}{\pi}\right). \tag{8.4}$$

Effectively this component establishes a positive gross investment benchmark that the 'profitability' components moderate. It means then that the profitability components may be symmetric with respect to rises and falls in gross investment, for the neutral position is this positive 'availability of finance' bench mark. As such we can speak of negative gross investment for the net effect after account is taken of the availability of finance element, is to make gross investment small or zero.[9] This expediency simplifies the mathematics considerably.

Profitability of expanding capacity

During a contraction, our model assumes (due to the complementarity between capacity, control and knowledge assets) that the level of (gross) capacity investment is zero. Equation (7.7a) represents the profit-maximising level of capacity investment when the aggregate level of economic activity it constant

$$I_{ca} = \left[\frac{1}{(1+z)^{\{1/1-\varepsilon\}}} \right] \left[\frac{\varepsilon}{(1+\lambda)\pi} \right]^{\{1/1-\varepsilon\}} \tag{7.7a}$$

and (7.5) represents the profit-maximising level of capacity investment during macroeconomic growth

$$I_{ca} = \left[\frac{\varepsilon}{(1+\lambda)\pi} \right]^{\{1/1-\varepsilon\}}. \tag{7.5}$$

When the optimal ratio of capital assets is in place and the level of profits is constant, firms merely invest for replacement purposes. Accordingly we may model I_{ca} as a positive function of the change in the level of aggregate profits. The sensitivity of I_{ca} to ΔP depends on the size of the expectations coefficient ε and the relative important of capacity investment to control and knowledge investment in the process of producing and selling commodities. The smaller is z and the larger is ε, the more sensitive I_{ca} is to ΔP. Formally we write

$$I_{ca} = b_0 + \frac{b_1}{\pi} \left(P^e_{t+1} - P_t \right) \tag{8.5}$$

where b_0 reflects δ_{ca}, b_1 reflects ε, and both vary indirectly with y and z.

Profitability of expanding knowledge and control assets
Equation (7.6) represents the profit-maximising levels of investment in knowledge and control assets during macroeconomic contraction

$$I_{kc} = \left[\frac{z}{z^{\{1/1-\varepsilon\}}} \right] \left[\frac{\varepsilon}{(1+\lambda)\pi} \right]^{\{1/1-\varepsilon\}}. \tag{7.6}$$

Equation (7.7b) represents the profit-maximising levels of investment in knowledge and control assets when economic activity is constant

$$I_{kc} = \left[\frac{z}{(1+z)^{\{1/1-\varepsilon\}}} \right] \left[\frac{\varepsilon}{(1+\lambda)\pi} \right]^{\{1/1-\varepsilon\}} \tag{7.7b}$$

and investment in knowledge and control assets is zero during macroeconomic growth. When the desired ratio of capital assets is attained and the level of profits is constant, firms will only investment for replacement purposes. Using a similar method as above we argue that knowledge and control investments are a negative function of the change in profitability. The smaller is the expectations coefficient ε and the less important control assets are to the process of producing and selling commodities (the smaller is y), the smaller is the absolute size of the coefficient relating I_{co} to ΔP. Formally we write

$$I_{co} = c_0 - \frac{c_1}{\pi} \left(P^e{}_{t+1} - P_t \right) \tag{8.6}$$

where c_0 reflects δ_{co}, c_1 reflects ε, and both vary directly with y and indirectly with z.

Full investment decision

If we assume the convention for determining profit expectations in the context of non-actuarial uncertainty, $P^e{}_{t+1} - P_t = P_t - P_{t+1}$, then the full *ex ante* investment decision (in linear difference format) is the sum of (8.4), (8.5) and (8.6)

$$I_{t+\tau} = \left[a_0 P_t + a_1 e^{a_2 t} \left(\frac{P_t}{\pi} \right) \right] + b_0 + \frac{b_1}{\pi} (P_t - P_{t-1}) + c_0 - \frac{c_1}{\pi} (P_t - P_{t-1}).$$

Aggregating and then combining this with Kalecki's macroeconomic relationship, $P_t = m(I_t + A_t)$, gives

$$I_{t+\tau} = m \left[a_0 + \frac{a_1 e^{a_2 t}}{\pi} + \frac{b_1 - c_1}{\pi} \right] I_t - m \left[\frac{b_1 - c_1}{\pi} \right] I_{t-1}$$

$$+ m \left[a_0 + \frac{a_1 e^{a_2 t}}{\pi} + \frac{b_1 - c_1}{\pi} \right] A_t - m \left[\frac{b_1 - c_1}{\pi} \right] A_{t-1} + (b_0 + c_0).$$

This may be simplified to

$$I_{t+\tau} = \rho\, I_t - \sigma\, I_{t-1} + \Phi = -(\sigma-\rho)\, I_t + \sigma\, \Delta I_t + \Phi. \qquad (8.7)$$

Where

$$\rho \;=\; m\!\left[a_0 + \left(a_1 e^{a_1 t} / \pi\right) + (b_1 - c_1)/\pi\right]$$

$$\sigma \;=\; m(b_1 - c_1 / \pi) \text{ and } \rho = \sigma - \rho = m(a_1 e^{a_1 t} / \pi)$$

$$\Phi \;=\; \rho A_t - \sigma A_{t-1} + B$$

$$B \;=\; b_0 + c_0.$$

The solution to equation (8.7) will yield a fluctuating pattern if $-(\sigma - \rho) < 1$. This is feasible and likely the smaller a_0 and a_1, the coefficients which represent the sensitivity of the investment decision to the firms estimated financial security.

The amplitude of oscillations will rise as σ rises.[10] The more sensitive investment on capacity capital is to the trade cycle relative to knowledge and control assets, the greater $(b_1 - c_1)$, the greater is the amplitude of fluctuations.

The same principle Kalecki used to solve his trend equation can be applied in this case. Assuming we can simplify $\Phi = q e^{\varphi t}$, the particular integral of (11.1) is

$$I^{cg} = \frac{\Phi}{e^{\varphi\tau} + \sigma - \rho - \sigma\varphi} = \frac{q e^{\varphi t}}{e^{\varphi\tau} + \sigma - \rho - \sigma\varphi} \qquad (8.8)$$

and

$$(e^{\varphi\tau} + \sigma - \rho - \sigma\varphi > 0).[11]$$

as $\sigma e^{-\varphi} = \sigma - \sigma\varphi$ when φ is very small. The *level* of I^{cg} and thus the extent to which the economy grows at a rate different to the full employment rate, depends on the size of q, due to the magnitudes of autonomous expenditures (A and B), and on the size of the coefficients which determine ρ and σ. Any once-off rise in the value of ρ or fall in σ will cause a once-off rise in the centre of gravitation both directly through the denominator of equation (8.8) and indirectly by increasing Φ and raising q.[12] The level of $(\sigma - \rho)$ depends on the access to finance variables and the level of B depends on the exogenous level of I_{kc} and I_{ca}. The rate of *growth* in the centre of gravitation, on the other hand, is represented by φ. It depends on the weighted *growth* of

A and B. It is not affected at all by the sensitivity of I_{kc} and I_{ca} to the trade cycle.

Conclusion

We have suggested that a successful macrodynamic relationship need only mimic the aggregate of all individual decisions at any point in time and allow for the macroeconomic consequences of this aggregate choice to feed into individual outcomes and then back into subsequent micro decisions. Once we have integrated our microeconomic decision function into a full macrodynamic model, we can analyse the effect a change in firms' desire to compete and change in their perception of uncertainty may have on the amplitude of trade cycle behaviour and the centre of gravitation around which the cycle fluctuates. This is not meant to represent a literal translation of the way an economy behaves but rather to illustrate developmental tendencies under a *ceteris paribus* method of analysis.

Notes

[1] In an open economy model with government, autonomous expenditures also include the government deficit and the current account surplus.

[2] $n\Delta P_t$ represents the part due to cyclical factors and δP_t represents the part due to the superior advantages embodied in the new asset.

[3] This effect of the expectation of future assets values is picked up by the second part of Kalecki's investment decision equation.

[4] Goudie and Meeks (1991) have found in their study using data from 975 firms that the five main financial variables (including the gearing ratio) explained 90 per cent of company failure in the UK between 1970–85.

[5] The default free central bank rate of interest is exogenous.

[6] Kalecki ([1939], 1990, 292). Carrington and Edwards (1979, 156) claim that it is usually more difficult to float new issues during recessions.

[7] Some theorists have argued that they will be more likely to manipulate the mark-up for this purposes. See Wood (1975), Harcourt and Kenyon ([1976], 1992).

[8] In our case this refers to the distribution of last periods profits and hence λ, and the relative sizes of π and ε.

[9] There are limits to this of course, extreme magnitudes of our coefficients will produce implausible results.

[10] The period also falls as σ rises.

[11] e here is the natural number not a coefficient.

[12] We can omit $\sigma\varphi$ from our calculations as it is very small.

9 Concluding Remarks

The genesis of scientific enquiry and analysis is usually the observation and interrogation of manifest phenomena. What we can see or feel grasps our earliest attention. Long before particle physics and gravity were even conceived, scientists were observing and theorising about the stars. Ailments were diagnosed and treated prior to any thought about the existence of the nervous system. Economics has not been different. Until a few decades ago there was little formal analysis of education, training, management, marketing or innovation, and most capital theory was concerned with the accumulation of material plant and equipment. Even today, only a limited part of our literature recognises the commonality between the separate intangible strands of economics.

In this book we have attempted to establish a case for taking more seriously than hitherto, the existence of a second type of enterprise capital. We have argued that the level of intangible investment and capital is non-trivial from both *a priori* and empirical perspectives. Our point is not so much whether knowledge, skills and organisation are becoming more important determinants of wealth and productivity, but whether these attributes are forming an increasing component of firm's investment activity. We have argued that intangible investment may be undertaken as part of the firm's drive to compete and also as part of the firm's need to contain its uncertainty about its internal and external markets. Given this, firms should continue to invest even during recessions, but we expect that the mix of these investments will vary over the trade (business) cycle.

If we accept that intangible capital is a significant and growing factor of production, then there are obvious implications for other areas of economics. First, the dominant capitalist form of ownership may not be an efficient ownership structure in industries where a significant part of the capital stock is unalienable from labour and synergies between labour. Firms from high technology, information technology and health service industries, which involve a high proportion of intangible capital, sell for considerable amounts of money when sold outright and also trade at very high price to NTA ratios. However, this can be a risky proposition, as some purchasers have discovered, if skilled workers leave or do not perform as expected. Multi-partnership structures, such as the traditional professional structure or other

101

forms of profit sharing may be more appropriate.¹ Conventional capitalist ownership structures may be increasingly limiting the size and efficiency of firms.

Second, we expect that firms with high levels of intangible capital will tend to encounter difficulties raising debt and will be forced to rely upon new share issues and retained earnings for investment finance. This may also artificially limit the investment rate and size of affected firms. Changes however, to the nature of company ownership may ameliorate this factor.

Third, if firms regard labour, in part, as raw investment material, then we expect, given the natural heterogeneity of individuals, that some labour will be highly prized and sought after for jobs that require capital investment while other labour will be considered unsuitable. 'Good' prospects are channelled into jobs, which strengthens their labour market position and 'poor' prospects will be relegated to the remaining jobs where development is not required. Farmers and land developers do not invest in land with poor potential even if the land is free. Similarly, no matter how low their wage, employers will not invest in a person who shows little promise of improvement. These processes will operate to polarise the labour market as those who are more skilled and motivated, those quicker to learn and communicate, and those who are able to work with others develop, leaving the rest of workers to jobs with little career path potential.

Finally, if these labour market processes are systematic and persistent, then there could be repercussions for income distribution. On the one hand incomes may converge, as a growing part of labour income includes capital income and the relative wealth derived from owning tangible capital falls. However, we may also see labour incomes diverge among the employed according to whether one gets a labour-as-capital job or a labour-as-input job. If employment opportunities in the non-asset labour market are consistently fewer than the number of workers excluded from the investment-assets sectors, a situation of chronic oversupply will develop. Of course, this chronic oversupply (unemployment) has existed in the western world for over two decades and in the US for longer, but it needs to be seen whether our theory of intangible capital can explain this phenomenon.

Notes

¹ The observed correlation between industry profits and wage rates may be attributable to some form of crude profit sharing arrangement in industry sectors where intangible capital is high rather than successful rent-seeking behaviour on behalf of unions.

References

Abramovitz M. (1993), 'The search for the sources of growth: Areas of ignorance, old and new', *Journal of Economic History*, **53**(2), 217–43.

Adams W.J. (1989), *Restructuring the French Economy*, Washington DC: The Brooking Institute.

Araujo L., Burrell G., Easton G., Rothschild R., Rothschild S. and Shearman C. (1989), 'Social approaches to the competitive process', in Francis A. and Tharakan P.K.M. (eds) (1989), pp. 137–64.

Arrow K.J. (1959), 'Toward a theory of price adjustment', *The Allocation of Economic Resources*, London, and Stanford: Stanford University Press, pp. 41–51.

Arrow K.J. ([1974a], 1984), 'Limited knowledge and economic analysis', *Economic Papers: The Economics of Information. Volume 4*, Oxford: Basil Blackwell, pp. 153–66.

Arrow K.J. ([1974b], 1984), 'On the agenda of organisations', *Economic Papers: The Economics of Information. Volume 4*, Oxford: Basil Blackwell, pp. 167–84.

Auerbach P. (1988), *Competition. The Economics of Industrial Change*, Oxford: Basil Blackwell.

Australian Stock Exchange Journal. (1972–1983, 1989), The Official Journal of The Australian Associated Stock Exchange. Sydney, Australia.

Bain J.S. ([1956], 1965), *Barriers to New Competition*, Cambridge Mass.: Harvard University Press.

Barth M.E. and Clinch G. (1998) 'Revalued financial, tangible and intangible assets: associations with share prices and non-market based value estimates', Working Paper, Graduate School of Business, Stanford University.

Best M.H. (1990), *The New Competition*, Cambridge: Polity Press.

Blanchard O.J. and Fischer S. (1989), *Lectures on Macroeconomics*, Cambridge, Mass.: MIT Press.

Borner S. (1989), 'Competitiveness and internationalisation of industry: The case of Switzerland', in Francis A. and Tharakan P.K.M. (eds) (1989), pp. 64–90.

Bos F. Holland. ïs H. and Keuning S.J. 'A Research and Development Module Supplementing the National Accounts' *Review of Income and Wealth,* **40**, 273–86.

Boulding K.E. (1950), *A Reconstruction of Economics,* NY: John Wiley and Sons.

Buckley P.J. (1985), 'A critical view of theories of the multinational enterprise', in Buckley P.J. and Casson M. (eds) *The Economic Theory of the Multinational Enterprise: Selected Papers,* London, Melbourne, Toronto: Macmillan, pp. 1–19.

Cantwell J. (1989), *Technological Innovation and Multinational Corporations,* Oxford: Basil Blackwell.

Carrington J.C. and Edwards G.T. (1979), *Financing Industrial Investment,* London and Basingstoke: Macmillan.

Caves R.E. and Murphy W.F. (1976) 'Franchising: Firms, markets and intangible assets', *Southern Journal of Economics,* **42**, 57–86.

Caves R.E. (1982a), *Multinational Enterprise and Economic Analysis,* Cambridge: Cambridge University Press

Caves R.E. (1982b), 'Multinational enterprises and technology transfer', in *New Theories of the Multinational Enterprise* Rugman A.M. (ed.) (1982) London, Canberra: Croom Helm, pp. 254–79.

Chamberlin E.H. ([1933], 1962), *The Theory of Monopolistic Competition,* Cambridge, Mass.: Harvard University Press, London: Oxford University Press, 8th edition.

Chandler A.D. and Hikino T. (1990), *Scale and Scope. The Dynamics of Industrial Capitalism,* Cambridge, Mass., London: Belknap Press of Harvard University.

Chauvin K.W. and Hirschey M. (1993) 'Advertising, R&D expenditure and the market value of the firm', *Financial Management,* Winter, 128–140.

Clark J.M. (1961), *Competition as a Dynamic Process,* Washington, DC: Brookings Institute.

Clifton J.A. (1977), 'Competition and the evolution of the capitalist mode of production', *Cambridge Journal of Economics,* **1**, 137–51.

Comanor W.S. and Wilson T.A. (1979), 'The effect of advertising on competition: A survey', *Journal of Economic Literature,* **17**(June), 453–76.

Cotter J. (1998), 'Asset revaluations and debt contracting', mimeo, University of Southern Queensland.

Deiaco E., Hörnell E. and Vickery G. (1990), *Technology and Investment Crucial Issues for the 1990s,* London: Pinter Publishers.

Demsetz H. (1982), 'Barriers to entry', *American Economic Review,* **72**(1), 47–57.

Dewey D.J. (1969), *The Theory of Imperfect Competition*, New York: Columbia University Press.

Dimbath E.F. (1994) 'The theory and practice determination of going concern value', *Journal of Forensic Economics,* **7**, 171–8.

Dixon R.J. (1986), 'Uncertainty, unobstructivness, and power', *Journal of Post-Keynesian Economics,* **8**(4), 585–90.

Doeringer P.B. and Piore M. (1971), *Internal Labour Markets and Manpower Analysis,* Lexington: Heath Lexington Books.

Doeringer P.B. and Terkla D.G. (1990), 'How intangible factors contribute to economic development: Lessons from a mature local economy', *World Development,* **18**(9), 1295–309.

Dolan E.G. (ed.) (1976), *The Foundations of Modern Austrian Economics,* Kansas City: Sheed and Ward.

Dosi G. (1988), 'Sources, procedures and microeconomic effects of innovation', *Journal of Economic Literature,* **26**(September), 1120–71.

Douglas P.H. ([1921], 1968) *American Apprenticeship and Industrial Education,* New York: AMS Press.

Doz Y. and Prahalad C.K. (1988), 'Quality of management: An emerging source of global competitive advantage', in Hood N. and Vahlne J.E. (eds) (1988), pp. 345–69.

Dunning J.H. (1988), 'International business, the recession and economic restructuring', in Hood N. and Vahlne J.E. (eds) (1988), pp. 84–103.

Eatwell J. (1987) 'Walras's theory of capital', in Eatwell J., Milgate M. and Newman P. (eds) (1987b), pp. 245–56.

Eatwell J., Milgate M., and Newman P. (eds) (1987a), *The New Palgrave: A Dictionary of Economics,* London and NY: Macmillan.

Eatwell J., Milgate M. and Newman P. (eds) (1987b), *The New Palgrave: Capital Theory,* London and Basingstoke: Macmillan.

Eisner R. (1989) *The Total Incomes System of Accounts,* Chicago and London: University of Chicago Press.

Eliasson G. (1988), *The Knowledge Base of an Industrial Economy,* The Industrial Institute for Economic and Social Research, Research Report 33, Stockholm.

Fisher I. (1930), *The Theory of Interest,* NY: Macmillan.

Ford J.L. (1994), *GLS Shackle. The Dissenting Economist's Economist.* Aldershot: Edward Edgar.

Ford J.L. (ed.) (1990), *Time, Expectations and Uncertainty in Economics. Selected Essays of GLS Shackle,* Aldershot: Edward Edgar.

Francis A. (1989), 'The concept of competitiveness', in Francis A. and Tharakan P.K.M. (eds) (1989), pp. 5–20.

Francis A. and Tharakan P.K.M. (eds) (1989), *The Competitiveness of European Industry,* London, New York: Routledge.

Freeman C. (1974), *The Economics of Industrial Innovation,* Harmondsworth: Penguin.

Fröhlich H.P. (1989), 'International competitiveness: Alternative macroeconomic strategies and changing perceptions in recent years', Francis A. and Tharakan P.K.M. (eds) (1989), pp. 21–40.

Garegnani P. (1987), 'Quantity of Capital', in Eatwell J., Milgate M. and Newman P. (eds) (1987b), pp. 1–78.

Geroski P.A. and Walters C.F. (1995), 'Innovative activity over the business cycle', *Economic Journal,* **105**, 916–28.

Gilbert R.J. (1989), 'Mobility barriers and the value of incumbency', in Schmalensee R. and Willig R.D. (eds) (1989), *Handbook of Industrial Organisation,* Amsterdam, New York, Oxford, Tokyo: North Holland, Volume I, pp. 475–535.

Goudie A.W. and Meeks G. (1991), 'Export and die: The exchange rate and company failure in a macro-micro model', *Economic Journal,* **101**(May), 444–57.

Grabowski H.G. and Mueller D.C. (1978), 'Industrial research and development, intangible capital stocks and firm profit rates', *Bell Journal of Economics,* **9**(2), 328–43.

Green H.A.J. (1977), 'Aggregation problems of macroeconomics', in Harcourt G.C. (1977), pp. 177–204.

Grossman G.M. and Helpman E. (1991), *Innovation and Growth in the Global Economy,* Cambridge, Mass: MIT Press.

Hahn F.H. and Hollis M. (eds) (1979), *Philosophy and Economic Theory,* Oxford: Oxford University Press.

Hamel G. and Prahalad C.K. (1988), 'Creating Global Strategic Capability' in Hood N. and Vahlne J.E. (eds), 1988, pp. 5–39.

Harcourt G.C. (1977), *The Microeconomic Foundations of Macroeconomics,* London, Basingstoke, Macmillan.

Harcourt G.C. (1994), 'What Adam Smith really said', *Economic Review,* **12**(2), 24–7.

Harcourt G.C. and Kenyon P. (1976), 'Pricing and the investment decision', in Sardoni C. (ed.) (1992), pp. 48–66.

Harrington J.E. (1987), 'Strategic behaviour and market structure', in Eatwell J., Milgate M. and Newman P. (eds) (1987a), Volume IV, pp. 513–15.

Hausman D.M. (ed.) (1984), *The Philosophy of Economics,* Cambridge: Cambridge University Press.

Hay D.A. and Morris D.J. (1991), *Industrial Economics and Organisation*, Oxford, Oxford University Press, second edition.

Hayek F.A. von (1941), *The Pure Theory of Capital*, London: Macmillan

Hayek F.A. von ([1946], 1949), 'The meaning of competition', in Hayek F.A. von, *Individualism and Economic Order*, London: Routledge and Kegan Paul.

Hayek F.A. von (1978), *New Studies in the Philosophy, Politics, Economics and the History of Ideas*, London, Henley: Routledge and Kegan Paul.

Hicks J.R. ([1946], 1986) 'Income', Parker R.H., Harcourt C.G. and Whittington G. (eds), (1986), *Readings in the Concept and Measurement of Incomes*, Oxford: Philip Alan, 102–10.

Hirschey M. (1982), 'Intangible capital assets of advertising and research and development expenditure', *Journal of Industrial Economics*, **30**(4), 175–90.

Hirshleifer J. (1976), *Price Theory and Applications*, New Jersey: Prentice-Hall.

Hood N. and Vahlne J.E. (eds) (1988), *Strategies in Global Competition*, London, New York, Sydney: Croom Helm.

Hymer S.H. ([1960], 1976), *The International Operations of National Firms: A Study of Direct Foreign Investment*, Cambridge, Mass: MIT Press.

Ioannides S. (1992), *The Market, Competition and Democracy*, Aldershot, UK and Brookfield, US: Edward Elgar.

Johansson J. and Mattsson L-G. (1988), 'Internationalisation in industrial systems – a network approach', in Hood N. and Vahlne J.E. (eds) (1988), pp. 287–314.

Jorgenson D.W. (1971), 'Econometric studies of investment behaviour: A survey', *Journal of Economic Literature*, **9**(4), 1111–47.

Kaldor N. (1950–51), 'The economic aspects of advertising' *Review of Economic Studies*, **XVIII**, 1–27.

Kalecki M. (1939), *Essays in the Theory of Economic Fluctuations*, in Osiatynski J. (ed.), (1990), pp. 233–318.

Kalecki M. (1940), 'The supply curve of an industry under imperfect competition', in Osiatynski J. (ed.) (1991), pp. 51–78.

Kalecki M. (1968), 'Trend and the business cycle', in Osiatynski J. (ed.) (1991), pp. 435–50.

Karlsson C. (1989), 'Hindering and supporting factors in the start-up of new, small technology based firms', in Francis A. and Tharakan P.K.M. (eds) (1989), pp. 91–109.

Kendrick J.W. (1972), 'The treatment of intangible resources as capital', *Review of Economic Studies*, **18**(1), 109–25.

Kendrick J.W. (1994) 'Total capital and economic growth', *Atlantic Economic Journal*, **22**, 1–18.

Keynes J.M. ([1936], 1973), *The General Theory of Employment, Interest and Money*, London and Basingstoke: Macmillan and Cambridge: Cambridge University Press for the Royal Economic Society.

Keynes J.M. (1937), 'The general theory of employment', *Quarterly Journal Of Economics*, **51**(February), 209–23.

Keynes J.N. (1917), 'The scope and method of political economy', in Hausman D.M. (ed.) (1984), pp. 70–98.

Kirzner I.M. (1969), 'Entrepreneurship and the market approach to development', in Kirzner I.M. (1979), *Perception, opportunity and profit*, Chicago, London: University of Chicago Press, pp. 107–119.

Kirzner I.M. (1973), *Competition and entrepreneurship*, Chicago, London: University of Chicago Press.

Kirzner I.M. (1976a), 'Economics and error', in Kirzner I.M. (1979), pp. 120–36.

Kirzner I.M. (1976b), 'On the method of Austrian economics', in Dolan E.G. (ed.) (1976), pp. 40–51.

Kirzner I.M. (1979) *Perception, opportunity and profit*, Chicago, London: University of Chicago Press.

Kirzner I.M. (1982), *Method, Process and Austrian Economics*, Lexington: DC Heath and co.

Knight F.H. ([1921], 1946), *Risk, Uncertainty and Profit*, Boston, New York: Houghton Mifflin company, The Riverside Press Cambridge.

Knight F.H. (1922), 'Ethics of the economic interpretation' in Knight F.H. (1935), pp. 17–40.

Knight F.H. (1923), 'The ethics of competition' in Knight F.H. (1935), pp. 41–75.

Knight F.H. (1924), 'The limitations of scientific method in economics', in Knight F.H. (1935), pp. 105–47.

Knight F.H. (1935), *The Ethics of Competition and Other Essays*, London: George Allen and Unwin.

Kogut B. (1988), 'Country patterns in international competition: Appropriability and oligopolistic agreement', in Hood N. and Vahlne J.E. (eds) (1988), pp. 315–40.

Kriesler P. (1989), 'Methodological implications of Kalecki's microfoundations', in Sebastiani M. (ed.) (1989), pp. 121–41.

Kurz H.D. (1987), 'Debates in capital theory' in Eatwell J., Milgate M. and Newman P. (eds) (1987b), pp. 79–93.

Lachmann L.M. (1986), *The Market as an Economic Process,* Oxford: Basil Blackwell.

Lamberton D.M. (1972), 'Information and profit', in Carter C.F. and Ford J.L. (eds) (1972), *Uncertainty and Expectations in Economics: Essays in Honour of GLS Shackle,* Oxford: Basil Blackwell, pp. 191–212.

Lavoie M. (1992), *Foundations of Post-Keynesian Economic Analysis,* Aldershot, UK and Brookfield, US: Edward Edgar.

Layard P.R.G., Nickell S. and Jackman R. (1991), *Unemployment: Macroeconomic Performance and the Labour Market,* Oxford, New York: Oxford University Press.

Lindbeck A. and Snower D. (1986), 'Wage setting, unemployment and insider-outsider relations', *American Economic Review,* **76,** 235–9.

Lipsey R.G. (1977), *An Introduction to Positive Economics,* London: Weidenfeld and Nicolson.

Loasby B.J. (1982), 'Economics of dispersed and incomplete information', in Kirzner I.M. (1982), pp. 111–30.

Loasby B.J. (1983), 'Knowledge, learning and enterprise', in, Wiseman J. (ed.) *Beyond Positive Economics,* London and Basingstoke: Macmillan, pp. 104–21.

Loasby B.J. (1991), *Equilibrium and Evolution,* Manchester, New York: Manchester University Press.

Magee S.P. (1977), 'Information and the multinational corporation: An appropriability theory of direct foreign investment', in Bhagwati J.N. (ed.), *The New International Economic Order,* Cambridge, Mass: MIT Press, pp. 317–40.

Markusen J.R. (1995), 'The boundaries of multinational enterprises and the theory of international trade', *Journal of Economic Perspectives,* **9**(2), 169–89.

Marshall A. ([1890], 1920), *Principles of Economics,* 8th edition, London: Macmillan.

Marshall A. ([1919], 1923), *Industry and Trade,* London: Macmillan.

Marx K. ([1894], 1972), *Capital. Volume III,* London: Lawrence and Wishart.

Matthews R.C.O. (1991), 'Animal spirits', in Meeks J.G.T. (ed.) (1991a), pp. 103–25.

McGee J. and Thomas H. (1988), 'Making sense of complex industries', in Hood N. and Vahlne J.E. (eds) (1988), pp. 40–78.

Meeks J.G.T. (ed.) (1991a), *Thoughtful Economic Man,* Cambridge: Cambridge University Press.

Meeks J.G.T. (1991b), 'Keynes on the rationality of decision procedures under uncertainty: the investment decision', Meeks J.G.T. (ed.) (1991a), pp. 126–60.

Megna P. and Klock M. (1993), 'The impact if intangible capital on Tobin's q in the semiconductor industry', *American Economic Review,* May (AEA Papers and Proceedings), 265–69.

Megna P. and Mueller D.C. (1989), 'Profit rates, intangibles capital and rent seeking', Working paper 89–14, University of Maryland, Department of Economics.

Mill J.S. (1836), 'On the definition and method of political economy', in Hausman D.M. (ed.) (1984), pp. 52–69.

Moir C. (1990), 'Competition in the UK grocery trades', in Moir C. and Dawson J. (eds) (1990), pp. 91–118.

Moir C. and Dawson J. (eds) (1990), *Competition and Markets,* London and Basingstoke: Macmillan.

Morck R. and Yeung B. (1991), 'Why investors value multinationality', *Journal of Business,* **64**(2), 165–87.

Morck R. and Yeung B. (1992), 'Internationalization. An event study test', *Journal of International Economics,* **33**, 41–56.

Myhrman J. (1989), 'The new institutional economics and the process of economic development', *Journal of Institutional and Theoretical Economics,* **145**(1), 38–59.

Nelson R.R. and Winter S.G. (1982), *An Evolutionary Theory of Economic Change,* Cambridge Mass., London: Belknap Press of Harvard University Press.

Odagiri H. (1992), *Growth through Competition, Competition through Growth,* Oxford: Clarendon Press.

Organisation for Economic Cooperation and Development (1979), *Trends in Industrial R and D in selected OECD member countries. 1965–1975,* Paris: OECD.

Organisation for Economic Cooperation and Development (1980), *Accounting Practices in OECD member countries,* Paris: OECD.

Organisation for Economic Cooperation and Development (1997), *Basic Science and Technology Statistics,* Paris: OECD.

Osiatynski J. (ed.) (1990), *Collected Works of Michal Kalecki, Volume I, Business Cycles and Full Employment,* Oxford: Clarendon Press.

Osiatynski J. (ed.) (1991), *Collected Works of Michal Kalecki, Volume II, Capitalism Economic Dynamics,* Oxford: Clarendon Press.

Pasinetti L.L. (1981), *Structural Change and Economic Growth,* Cambridge: Cambridge University Press.

Penrose E.T. ([1959], 1980), *The Theory of the Growth of the Firm*, Oxford: Basil Blackwell.

Pesaran M.H. (1987), *The Limits to Rational Expectations,* Oxford: Basil Blackwell.

Pettigrew A., Whipp R. and Rosenfeld R. (1989), 'Competitiveness and the management of strategic change processes', in Francis A. and Tharakan P.K.M. (eds) (1989), pp. 110–36.

Porter M.E. (1990), *The Competitive Advantage of Nations,* London, Basingstoke: Macmillan.

Ray T., Evans J., Boden M., Metcalfe J.S. and Gibbons M. (1989), 'Competition and the momentum of technical change', in Francis A. and Tharakan P.K.M. (eds) (1989), pp. 165–99.

Reid G.C. (1989), *Classical Economic Growth. An Analysis in the Tradition of Adam Smith,* Oxford: Basil Blackwell.

Richardson G.B. ([1960], 1990), *Information and Investment,* Oxford: Clarendon Press.

Robinson J. ([1933], 1969), *The Economics of Imperfect Competition,* London: Macmillan, St Martin's Press, 2nd edition.

Robinson J. ([1956], 1966), *The Accumulation of Capital,* London, Melbourne and Toronto: Macmillan.

Romer P.M. (1986), 'Increasing returns and long-run growth', *Journal of Political Economy,* **94**(5), 1002–37.

Romer P.M. (1990), 'Endogenous technical change', *Journal of Political Economy,* **98** (5 pt 2), s71–s102.

Rothschild K.W. (1942), 'A note on advertising' *Economic Journal,* **52,** April, 112–21.

Rothschild K.W. (1947), 'Price theory and oligopoly' *Economic Journal,* **57,** September, 299–320.

Rugman A.M. (1981), 'Internationalisation as a general theory of foreign direct investment: A re–appraisal of the literature', *Weitwirtschaftliches Archiv,* **116**, 365–75.

Sardoni C. (ed.) (1992), *On Political Economists and Modern Political Economy: Selected Essays of G.C. Harcourt,* London and NY: Routledge.

Sargent T.J. (1987), *Macroeconomic Theory,* Boston: Academic Press.

Sawyer M.C. (1989), *The Challenge of Radical Political Economy: An Introduction to the Alternative to Neo-classical Economics,* NY: ME Sharpe and London, Toronto, Sydney, Tokyo: Harvester Wheatsheaf.

Schreyer P. and Clark W.S. (1991), 'Intangible investment and current tax reforms', *Canadian Journal of Economics,* **24**(4), 873–87.

Schumpeter J.A. ([1911], 1934), *The Theory of Economic Development,* translated by R. Opie, Cambridge, Mass.: Harvard University Press, Harvard Economic Studies, Volume XLVI (original in German).

Scitovsky T. (1992), *The Joyless Economy,* Oxford, New York: Oxford University Press, revised edition.

Sebastiani M. (ed.) (1989), *Kalecki's Relevance Today,* NY: St Martin's Press

Shackle G.L.S. (1942), 'A theory of investment decisions', in Ford J.L. (ed.) (1990), pp. 103–20.

Shackle G.L.S. (1943), 'The exceptational dynamics of the individual', in Ford J.L. (ed.) (1990), pp. 51–129.

Shackle G.L.S. (1956), 'Expectations and cardinality', in Ford J.L. (ed.) (1990), pp. 82–90.

Shackle G.L.S. (1961–62), 'The description of uncertainty', in Shackle G.L.S. (1966), pp. 85–99.

Shackle G.L.S. (1966), *The Nature of Economic Thought,* Cambridge: Cambridge University Press.

Shares. Your Guide to Australia's Best Stocks. (1990–1998). Melbourne, Australia.

Simon H.A. (1976), 'From substantive to procedural rationality', in Hahn F.H. and Hollis M. (eds) (1979), pp. 65–86.

Slatter S. St P. (1977), *Competition and Marketing Strategies in the Pharmaceutical Industry,* London: Croom Helm.

Smith A. ([1776] 1976), *An Inquiry into the Nature and Causes of The Wealth of Nations,* edited by E. Cannan, Chicago: University of Chicago Press.

Stock Exchange of Melbourne. Official Record. (1947–1971), Committee of the Stock Exchange of Melbourne.

Teece D.J. (1977), 'Technology transfer by multinational firms, the resource cost of transferring technological know-how', *Economic Journal,* **87**(June), 242–61.

Telser L.G. (1961), 'How much does it pay whom to advertise', *American Economic Review,* **51**(supplement), 194–205.

Torr C. (1988), *Equilibrium, Expectations and Information,* Cambridge: Polity Press.

White F.C. (1995), 'Valuation of intangible capital in agriculture', *Journal of Agricultural and Applied Economics,* **27**, 437–45.

Wood A. (1975), *A Theory of Profits,* Cambridge: Cambridge University Press.

Young A. (1928), 'Increasing returns and economic progress', *Economic Journal,* **38**, December, 527–42.

Index

NEW DIRECTIONS IN MODERN ECONOMICS